Kingston

Then and Now

Kingston
Then and Now

*A Loyal Tribute for the Silver Jubilee
of Queen Elizabeth II*

MARGARET BELLARS

Michael Lancet
PUBLISHER & BOOKSELLER

Dr. E. M. LANCET
Esher, Surrey

©Margaret Bellars, 1977
ISBN 0 900245 09 3

Printed by South London Press.

CONTENTS

    List of Illustrations ....

    Preface ....

    Introduction ....

1. Kingston 1
2. Surbiton 25
3. Malden and Coombe 49

ILLUSTRATIONS

1. The Coronation Stone, Kingston High Street
2. All Saints Church, Kingston
3. Kingston Market Place
4. Regatta Day, Canbury Gardens
5. The Bandstand, Canbury Gardens
6. Seaplane testing, near Canbury Gardens
7. Queen Victoria's Jubilee Fountain
8. Raven's Ait, Surbiton
9. Electric Parade, Brighton Road, Surbiton
10. St Mark's Church, Surbiton
11. Tolworth Fountain
12. Coronation Clocktower, Surbiton
13. Ewell Road, Surbiton
14. The Bonesgate, Chessington
15. A cottager's stall
16. Oil Mill Lane, Kingston
17. The Fountain, Malden
18. Christ Church, New Malden, as planned
19. Malden's first Wesleyan Chapel
20. Malden Council outing
21. Trams at Eden Street junction, Kingston
22. Luxury tram, London Road
23. Flood trams, Burlington Road
24. Cheamside, Worcester Park

PREFACE

We, the Queen's Silver Jubilee Mayors of the Royal Borough of Kingston upon Thames, welcome this Kingston, Surbiton and Malden account compiled by Margaret Bellars. It reflects the Borough's growth. We are justifiably proud of our past and look forward with confidence to the future.

Those who were born in the area will find memories they can share. To newcomers, the details will be enthralling.

Councillor Frank Steptoe, Mayor 1976–77

Alderman Doris Tapping, Mayor 1977–78

Introduction

For some four hundred years the name Queen Elizabeth has been specially revered in Kingston.

Accompanied by her Court, the great Tudor Queen Elizabeth I would ride from her royal Palace of Hampton Court across Kingston's ancient wooden bridge to receive the homage of her loyal citizens in the bustling market town. On 19th June 1917, Kingston re-enacted one of these royal processions in aid of comforts for the troops in the first world war. Dr W. S. St Lawrence Finny, seven times Mayor of Kingston, was Pageant Master. Queen Elizabeth I, riding at the head of the state procession, was represented by the Marchioness of Townshend.

Queen Elizabeth Grammar School, the original name for Kingston Grammar School, London Road, was founded in 1561 at the direct command of Queen Elizabeth I, and in 1961 Queen Elizabeth II came on a visit to Kingston to mark the 400th anniversary of the founding of Kingston Grammar School by her royal predecessor.

This account, in 1977, of how Kingston has grown since the 1887 days of Queen Victoria's Golden Jubilee is a loyal offering for Queen Elizabeth II's Silver Jubilee.

The original articles republished here formed a series, starting January 1972, in the Kingston Borough News, owned from 1963 until January 1977 by Haywill Press Ltd., Streatham.

This firm has now been responsible for the printing of this Jubilee edition, published by Dr Michael Lancet, publisher and bookseller of Esher and Surbiton. The present owners of the Kingston Borough News, the Argus Press Ltd., have offered every encouragement. Mrs Cathy Bradley has skilfully prepared the book for printing.

To all those readers of the Kingston Borough News whose memories and loaned photographs have made this book possible, my devoted and heartfelt thanks.

Margaret Bellars
May 1977

1. KINGSTON

The High Street

At one time Kingston High Street was called West-by-Thames Street but by 1887 it had achieved High Street name and status. Life in Kingston was then still at the horse-and-cart pace. The list of traders in the High Street, as late as 1902, recalls a now-vanished era when silk top hats were ordinary commodities offered for sale. Licences for keeping male servants and for armorial bearings were procurable at local post offices.

My guide to these early days has been Mr Sammy Emms (95), for over fifty years President of the Kingstonian Football Club. Sammy was born in December 1881, at 31 Market Place, Kingston. His father kept a prosperous saddlery and harnessmaker's shop.

Along Kingston High Street, going east towards Kingston Bridge from Town's End Wharf (now a public pleasure garden), we begin with the Anglers Public House. It was into the river opposite this pub that water for Hampton Court Palace was pumped from Cardinal Wolsey's Coombe Hill Conduit Houses. Having crossed the Fairfield, the water passed in two sets of pipes to Hampton Court Home Park via the river bed. This continued until the 1880s when a boat fouled the pipes—and broke the "silver" stream which came to Coombe Hill from the Whipsnade area via the London clay belt.

A little further along from the Anglers was Coldwell's Servants Registry, Stationers and Riverside Post Office. Next door was the premises of a coal merchant, Mr Thomas C. Smith, Mayor of Kingston from 1927-8.

At the corner of the High Street and East Lane, now Moss Brothers, outfitters, was Joe M. Wilcox & Son, Butchers. Their shop displayed the Royal Crest by appointment to Queen Victoria and Prince Albert at Claremont, Esher. Today, Wilcox Automobiles Ltd., on the opposite side of the High Street, still bears the family name.

At 35 High Street there was an internationally famous china shop kept by a remarkable broken-china repairer, Mr Thomas Abbott, grandfather of today's Kingston Councillor Mrs Dorothy Judge. The Pottery Gazette of 1909 stated: "In 1889, he deliberately broke a ewer into 289 pieces. He then, as a hobby, restored this by using 613 rivets. This ewer is displayed at Kingston Museum. He also made a crazy patchwork vase out of 1,540 small pieces of china. During the early 1900s, he was commissioned to repair a number of items from the famous Imperial Russian dinner service comprising 952 pieces, bearing 1,282 painted views of Great Britain. This service was made in 1774 for Empress Catherine II by Wedgewood's."

At 36 High Street was Willinghams, rod and tackle makers: "flies of every description made to pattern." 11 High Street housed Coppinger's distillery, next door was the home of E. T. Coppinger. This was beside the Hogsmill river and occupied the site of the present Kingston Police Station, headquarters of London's "V" Division.

Clattern House, on the site of today's Guildhall, was Council offices, numbering among its officials an Inspector of Nuisances. It also housed Kingston's first free public library, opened in 1882, which contained some 12,000 volumes.

The Market Place

In 1902 about forty businesses constituted Kingston's bustling Market Place. The stalls in the centre were only erected on specified days. When not in use the tackle needed was kept in the ground floor of the Town Hall, now the Market House.

Until 1935, when the present Guildhall in the High Street was opened by Princess Alice of Athlone, the Council meetings were held in the Italian-styled Town Hall, built in 1840 at a cost of some £4,000 to a plan prepared by a Mr C. Henmann. The gilded statue of Queen Anne, cast in lead, was placed on the front balcony to perpetuate the memory of one of the most prosperous periods of Kingston's history. This statue, designed by Francis Bird and erected in 1706, originally adorned Kingston's Tudor Market Hall.

A series of six handsome stained-glass windows, telling of the town's traditions, illumined the Town Hall Council Chamber, today used for the meetings of various societies. The windows were specially designed by Dr W. S. St Lawrence Finny, seven times Mayor of Kingston. Because of the difference in architectural proportions and because the rich patterns on the windows tended to obscure the light, the windows are now in the Kingston Museum and Library complex, Fairfield.

It was on the steps of the old Town Hall that each year's mayor stood on Shrove Tuesday to watch Kingston's historic "football" game, thought by some to be the origin of today's world-wide sport.

The Hock Tuesday (Shrove Tuesday) game symbolised a tradition handed down for four hundred years. Historians give at least two possible origins. The first commemorates a defeat sustained by the Danes at the hands of Kingston townfolk. The Danes' captain was slain. In commemoration of the victory, his head, in the form of a "football," was kicked about by opposing teams of townspeople. The "pitch" was from Clattern Bridge to Kingston Bridge by way of the

Market Place and Thames Street. One side represented Kingstonians of the day. The other represented the Danes.

The second legend states that in the year 754 or 755, Kenulf, king of one of the minor Saxon tribes, was lured by a beautiful maid to visit Merton. There he was treacherously slain by Kynard, the area leader. In revenge, Kingston people armed and hastened to Merton. They defeated the forces of the assassin and carried off the villain's head in triumph. This head is given as another origin of the "football."

Over the years, the Shrovetide football game grew increasingly rowdy. Public houses did a roaring trade but shops were forced to barricade their windows. In an attempt to preserve order, the game was shifted to the Fairfield in 1860. It lost favour with the change of venue and was suppressed seven years later.

A major force among the Market Place business premises of the nineteenth century was the Shrubsole Bank, founded in 1792. It amalgamated in 1894 with Parr's Banking Company, the Shrubsole family retaining a big interest in the bank and in Kingston's welfare. Today its premises are occupied by the National Westminster Bank, Market Place. Henry Shrubsole was elected Kingston's Mayor three times (in 1877, 1878 and 1879). He died suddenly in his third term of office while presiding at a Christmas charity dinner in the Drill Hall, then in Orchard Road. In recognition of his public services, the now-disused Shrubsole fountain was erected in Kingston Market Place. It cost some £500 and was carved from a block of Sicilian marble by Mr J. J. Williamson of Esher. The fountain was dedicated on 1 May 1882, by H.R.H. George, Duke of Cambridge, the most important landowner in Coombe.

At No. 5 Market Place was Chilcott Bros, tailors, specialists in riding habits. Jimmy Chilcott was the champion figure skater for miles around. There was plenty of ice in those days. Winters were hard and summers were hot. Some seven or eight weeks skating was available almost every year. On winter's evenings, the Long Water at Hampton Court Palace Home Park was lit up by fairy lights, contrived by standing a lighted candle in a mixture of sand and earth. Men had regular pitches for their booths at which clients paid to sit on a chair when changing into their skates. Every October, Kingston's pawn shops used to put out strings of skates of all types.

It was said that a tunnel emerged into the basement of Chilcott's premises, passing under the Thames from Hampton Court. Tradition says it was wide enough to permit the passage of a coach and was used by King Henry VIII on nocturnal expeditions.

The focus of entertainment was at No. 10 Market Place, the now-vanished Sun Hotel, superseded on the site by Woolworth's store today. The Sun was a centre of gaiety in Kingston until the late 1920s. It was auctioned for redevelopment in 1931. The Sun's river gardens were the favourite place for watching Kingston's annual regatta and regular concert parties attracted large open-air audiences throughout the summer.

The Griffin Hotel, at the other end of the Market Place, today links past and present. The former entrance to the hotel's famed Assembly Rooms is now the Ballroom and Banqueting Hall entrance. Built in Tudor times during the reign of King Edward VI (1537-53) The Griffin retained its sixteenth century appearance until the early nineteenth century.

A popular host at The Griffin was John Williams, twice Mayor of Kingston (1858 and 1864). He was a great character. When he was to be presented at Court to Queen Victoria, he had a Court dress tailormade and procured a Court sword. On the eve of the presentation, he held a reception at his private house in St James's Road and appeared in full Court dress to the admiration of his many friends.

The Royal Crest of the Griffin Hotel facade recalls the inn's association with the Royal Mail coaches. Kingston Market Place was a regular stopping place on the London to Portsmouth route. At one time twenty-six coaches passed through Kingston daily on scheduled routes; Kingston was a fare stage.

Today's Griffin Hotel, refurbished in regal splendour, is a fitting background for local royal Silver Jubilee celebrations.

In pride of place in Kingston is the famous Coronation Stone, crowning place by tradition of at least seven Anglo-Saxon kings. This stone, lost for generations, was discovered in a neglected state in the Corporation yard at the rear of Clattern House. Its varied career had included a sojourn in the porch of Kingston Grammar School, a period on Kingston waterfront and use as a mounting block near the Market Place Town Hall.

In September 1850, the Stone's wandering days were over. With great ceremony, it was placed in the centre of Kingston High Street, between The Griffin and Clattern House. The Provincial Grand Master of the Freemasons officiated before Kingston city fathers and a large crowd of interested onlookers, and anointed the Stone with oil and wine.

The base on which the Stone is set records the names, in Saxon spelling, of the seven kings said to have been crowned upon it: Edward the Elder, son of Alfred the Great (900), Athelstan (925), Edmund (940), Edred (946), Edwy (956), Edward the Martyr (975) and Ethelred II (979). A silver penny of the reign of each of these kings is set into the plinth of the Stone.

When traffic problems grew more acute in Kingston, the Coronation Stone was moved to its present position on a lawn before the Guildhall.

For generations, Kingston townsfolk have passed through Kingston Market Place or up Church Street, originally Church Row, to worship at All Saints Church.

Fig. 1. The Coronation Stone, Kingston High Street.

Fig. 2 All Saints Church, before the churchyard was grassed over.

KINGSTON

Today's Kingston War Memorial Gardens, Church Street, were once the parish church "overflow" churchyard. They were laid out in 1823 for this purpose. This "New Burial Ground", as it was called, became full comparatively soon. In 1854, a cemetery of about twenty-five acres was laid out on Bonner Hill, Norbiton. This ground was purchased for £7,000, and large sums must have since been spent on it and on additional land. In the 1900s, the burial ground between Church Street and Union Street, formerly called Brick Lane because of the brickfields in the area, lay behind a high iron railing with imposing pillars as gateposts. At either end of this frontage were two remarkable buildings of which one (now the Danish food shop) survives today. Until comparatively recently, it was the House of Gausten, tailors, but originally it was the Watch House of Kingston's early fire fighters. In the early days, it had no upper storey.

Later it was the town's mortuary. "When I was a lad," Sammy Emms recalled, "there were quite often drownings in the Thames. We lads would often go fishing. We would see a body coming down river. If it were taken ashore on the Surrey side, the men would get half-a-crown. If it were brought ashore on the Middlesex side, they got seven-and-sixpence. So they used to push it over to the other bank and then pull it ashore. We would watch the police ambulance—a handcart covered with a black hood—go over the bridge. The word would get around and there would usually be some thirty or forty kids gathered outside the mortuary to see the corpse brought in."

The building's vanished partner was the fire-engine shed. Local authorities were empowered by a *Lighting and Watching Act* to organise night patrols to watch for fires, to supply and maintain fire appliances and places to keep them, and to pay proper persons to look after fire-fighting equipment.

The "steamer" fire engine, first used in 1830, consisted of a horse-drawn vehicle on which was mounted a ten-horse-power steam-driven pump. Kingston had a "steamer" according to old records. It was not until 1903 that bells were introduced on most fire engines, so the firemen cleared a way with a cry of "Hi-ya-hi" copied, it was said, from the rope-hauling shanty-call of seamen, for ex-sailors were the usual source of recruitment for fire-fighting services.

Can you imagine the scene on a winter's night—men of the Watch shouting, the horses eager to be off, Kingston's gallant firemen scrambling to their places with the "steamer" and then off with a shout and a flourish.

The lot of Kingston firemen at the turn of the century was, however, far from happy. This is clear from a statement made by Mr F. J. Bell, Captain of the Brigade, at a quarterly meeting of Kingston, Surbiton and District Fire Brigade Committee held at Clattern House (then the Municipal Offices) in February 1899. After stating that his brigade had been called out on sixteen occasions since the committee last met, he drew their attention to a vital deficiency—the poor water supply. It was no use calling a fire engine to a fire, he said, if on arrival at the flames, the men could find no suitable water supply and had to stand there idle, the laughing stock of large crowds.

The Watch House was the duty room of the Watchmen of the Borough. They used to assemble clad in grey greatcoats in winter, muffled up to their ears, carrying stout sticks or bludgeons and equipped with horn "lanthorns" lighted with tallow candles.

Much of Kingston's commercial prosperity, so far as shoppers are concerned, has been bound up in the town's right to hold street markets by Royal Charter, granted by King Charles I in 1628.

This charter states: "We do grant to the same Bailiffs and their successors that no other market shall from henceforth in future be created anew, or in any manner appointed, or any way held in any place whatsoever within the distance of seven miles from the aforesaid town of Kingston upon Thames."

Three markets constitute Kingston's street-trading "kingdom." These are the daily trading in the town's Market Place, before Kingston Market Hall, and in the Apple Market, and the Monday market in Fairfield Municipal Car Park.

The Apple Market is connected to Church Street by Crown Passage and to the Market Place by Harrow Passage. Iron bollards, ornamented with the town's three-salmon crest, are used to permit only pedestrians to use the passages. The bollards were made at Harrison's foundry, once in Kingston High Street.

Around the 1900s the Brethren Gospel Hall was at No. 4 Apple Market. The premises also housed the Provident Dispensary Board Room. The desire of that Board was "to ensure to the working classes and their families efficient medical advice and medicine during illness." This was, in effect, Kingston's National Heath Service on a small scale. In those days, considerable poverty—and drunkenness, with children hanging about the public houses—was commonplace.

That the public conscience was disturbed by these conditions is suggested by the number of religious meeting houses in Kingston at that time. Beside the established churches and the Salvation Army, there were three in the centre of Kingston: the Brethren Gospel Hall (seating 180) in the Apple Market, another in St. James's Road (seating 100) and one in Fife Road (seating 120). Twice a week, the Salvation Army, with their band, held services lasting an hour and a half in the Apple Market.

Brook Street

A big step in Kingston's progress came in 1875 with the construction of the town's first purpose-built post office, at the corner of

Brook Street and Eden Street. Earlier, the post office had been in a grocer's shop next to the Griffin Hotel and earlier still on the opposite side of Kingston Market Place.

One of the most important businesses in Brook Street at the turn of the century was Arminger and Russell, dyers and cleaners, at Nos. 9, 11 and 13. In those days, the aristocracy's ball gowns and long white evening gloves featured in local trade. The next major premises along Brook Street on the post office side was the showroom and forge of Jacob Batson, wheelwright. This Brook Street business had opened in 1738. The Batson family came into the concern some hundred years later. Mr Eric Batson—central Kingston's last blacksmith—retired in 1971.

Soon after he retired, Mr Batson told me: "In my grandfather's time we built for special orders as well as for local traders. We supplied water-carts for Kingston Corporation because the streets were so dusty in those days. We developed the engineering side. The forge was always at the rear. My first job, as a lad straight from school, was to put the holes in horseshoes destined for the Russian front in the 1914–18 war. My dad took me up to London when he went to sign the contract with the Government for supplying horseshoes. They were a special heavy type with six holes in each side for quick fitting. Hundreds of horses were used in that war, of course, and thousands of horseshoes were supplied by blacksmiths.

"In those days it was a seven-year apprenticeship for the blacksmith's trade. Then the apprentice became a journeyman with his own kit and tools. The name meant he could journey from place to place gaining experience. It was a sixty-hour week then with some wages being at around 6d. an hour."

In those days, Brook Street ended with the Hogsmill Watersplash, correctly known as Bedelsford (now the Bedelsford Bridge), just after the junction of Brook Street with Orchard Road. This was beloved by boys who used to climb on the railings of the pedestrian footway. Dray horses trundled through it from Hodgson's Kingston Brewery; these premises are now the site of a major office block and a multi-shopping complex, occupying the land between Brook Street and St. James's Road. Hodgson's brewery was a flourishing family business. In the year 1897–8, it produced some 1,440,000 gallons of beer and employed sixty men. Earlier the brewery was owned by the Rowlls family, after whom Rowlls Road, Kingston, is named.

Until comparatively recently the Tiffin Girls School, built in 1899 at a cost of £12,000, stood in St James's Road. The site is now part of Kingston College of Further Education. Before their school was built, Tiffin girls shared with Tiffin boys the school by the Fairfield now occupied by St Joseph's Roman Catholic Primary School. Tiffin Girls School is now in Richmond Road, Kingston.

The next building of educational importance in the St James's

Road area in 1900 was the Art School and Technical College, now rebuilt as part of Kingston College of Further Education. The original premises cost £7,700 to build and was opened in February 1899 by the Lord Chief Justice Lord Russell of Killowen, who was entertained to a civic luncheon at St. James's Hall.

The record of the hall itself is remarkable. It was the meeting place of the Kingston Good Templars' Lodges, including the Lily of the Valley Juvenile Temple, the Kingston Literary Society and, on Saturday nights, popular entertainment concerts were run by the Kingston-on-Thames Total Abstinence Society.

Thames Street

A puzzle awaits us at the point where Thames Street leaves Kingston Market Place. Early photographs show two iron bollards, one each side of the roadway; between them is a cobbled strip—just like a pedestrian crossing. And, indeed, that is what it was; this type of cobbled footway crossed a number of Kingston streets at that time. In the summer, surfaces were so dusty despite frequent watering, that people preferred to cross on the cobbles. In bad weather, this was even more desirable.

One of the Thames Street bollards still remains today. Were they originally gun barrels brought by Kingston Corporation after the Crimean War? Some older residents believe they were. A cannonball, they say, rests in the muzzle.

King's Passage and Bishop's Hall are two excitingly named routes to the Thames from Thames Street. I believe it was down King's Passage in 1377 that ten-year-old King Richard II left Kingston to journey by water to London to ascend the throne following the death of his grandfather Edward III. He had been brought to Kingston for his education by his mother, Joan, Maid of Kent, after the death of his father, the Black Prince. Another explanation of the name could be that it was the route to the State barge used by King John, who reigned 1199–1216. A column, said to be from King John's Kingston Palace, once in the region of Clattern Bridge (Kingston High Street) can be seen in the grounds of Kingston Central Library, Fairfield.

King's Passage and Bishop's Hall remain, but Fountain Yard, later called Fountain Court, a fascinating backwater off Thames Street, has vanished. It was once an oasis of peace, entered between Nos. 27 and 29 Thames Street. Six addresses of private houses in Fountain Court are given in records. A watercolour of Fountain Court painted in 1913 shows the old stonework mellowed in the golden light of a summer afternoon, window boxes abloom and creepers gracing red-brick and yellow-stone walls; a scene worthy of a cathedral city. In the centre of the Court was an old pump and an ancient well.

Eden Street

Eden Street, known as Heathen Street on earlier maps, had become a "white collar" area of Kingston by the 1900s.

Eden Lodge, No. 59, was the home of Dr W. G. Crewell, an esteemed physician. The Primrose League, Kingston Habitation No. 374, was at No. 51. Dr Albion P. Alderson, musician and organist at All Saints Church, was at Dunelm, No. 47. The secretary to the Trustees of Kingston-on-Thames Municipal Charities, Mr J. Bedford Marsh, had his offices at Marsh, Sherwood and Hart in Eden Street. The charities are now known as Kingston upon Thames United Charities. Their provisions include funds for Cleaves Almshouses and the Countess of Dover's gift in perpetuity. By a deed dated 6 December 1664, the countess gave from the rents of her lands in Southwark a yearly sum £5 4s., for ever to be expended on bread and distributed in Kingston by the Vicar and Churchwardens on Lord's Day each week for the use and relief of the poor. Two dozen loaves weekly was the amount suggested for distribution.

Towards the end of Eden Street was a cut through towards Clarence Street. It was called Young's Buildings Passage. The Buildings themselves were demolished prior to the construction of today's multi-storey Eden Street car park.

Many will remember Young's Buildings. They were a row of thirteen three- or four-storey terraced houses fronting straight on to a narrow pavement. The continuation from the houses to Clarence Street (this still exists today) was called Pratt's Alley: it is the narrow footpath by Marks and Spencer's store, Clarence Street.

In the 1900s the Buildings were the "Gorbals" of Kingston. By the 1940s they had smartened up considerably and many had splendid windowboxes to compensate for a lack of front gardens.

In the old days, it was children from those buildings who thronged to the "sparrows breakfasts" given at the Three Compasses public house, Eden Street, for a number of years.

In addition to the cheap food at the breakfasts, provided because in many cases both parents were at work, an annual "sparrows dinner" was held at the New Year in the Drill Hall, Orchard Road. Mr William Crow, then licensee of the Three Compasses, was on the organising committee. His wife presided over one of the five long tables needed to accommodate the five hundred boys and girls entertained, with boys on one side of the hall and girls on the other, a hundred to a table. After a roast beef and plum pudding dinner, the children were entertained with a Punch and Judy show, a concert and games. These included tug-of-war with a monster bon-bon, 12 ft long and 4 ft across. When it exploded, large quantities of low-value coins were scattered among the children. Each child was given a warm woollen wrapper on going home and 1,000 boxes of sweets and 1,000 oranges, gifts from traders, were distributed.

Kingston tannery, which flourished off Bishop's Hall, was closed in May 1963, having been in business on the site for 170 years. Demolition took place almost immediately and on 10 June the site was devastated by fire. For years, Kingstonians had been complaining of the smell of curing leather when the wind was in an unfavourable direction. The stench on 10 June, when a pall of black smoke covered the town, was indescribable.

The Congregational Church (now the United Reformed Church), Eden Street, has today been preserved externally as a fine example of the best Victorian architecture in Kingston. It was built in 1855–6 at a cost of £4,500. The church was originally founded by the Rev. Richard Mays, one-time vicar of All Saints, Kingston Parish Church. He was deprived of his All Saints living in 1662 under the *Act of Uniformity*. He died in 1695 and there is a tablet to his memory in the South Chancel of All Saints Church.

Also in Eden Street is the Friends Meeting House, an important building in the spiritual development of Kingston, a noted dissenters' town. Originally the Meeting House had a formal garden surrounding the present central section. A remarkable handwritten account of the Friends' work in Kingston was lent to me some years ago by the late Mr Albert Harris of Grand Avenue, Tolworth. He died comparatively recently in his nineties. His father, born in 1817, two years after the Battle of Waterloo, was treasurer of the Kingston Society of Friends for a number of years. He wrote his account of their work soon after 1850. A copy is now in the archives of Kingston Central Library.

Continuing along Eden Street, the section just prior to Kingston Market Place was once known as Gigg's Hill and the alley now known as Bath Passage was known as Gigg's Hill Passage. The name changed when public baths were opened there in 1852 for the benefit of poorer citizens. They were called St James's Baths and were "admirably fitted and accessible at a low charge," states an 1877 record, adding "after languishing for a few years, the baths were closed."

Kingston Bridge

Seventeen years before Queen Victoria's Golden Jubilee (1887), on 12 March 1870, toll charges on Kingston Bridge were repealed for ever. The ceremony of "freeing" the bridge was performed by the Lord Mayor of London amid amazing scenes of rejoicing.

An Act of Parliament was needed to bring "free trade" to the town. It was, in fact, the second time the tolls had been abolished: the first was in 1565 when Robert Hammond, a prosperous Kingston citizen, settled land to the value of £40 a year for the future support of the town's wooden bridge and for its exemption from tolls. Much of Kingston's market prosperity was due to this citizen's far-sighted charity.

However, by the 1800s, Kingston desperately needed a new bridge. The Town Council of the day took steps to reimpose toll charges to pay for a bridge "chaste and elegant in design."

This bridge, substantially as it is today (it was widened in 1912–14), was designed by Mr Edward Lapidge. The cost, including the approach roadways, was £40,000. The first stone was laid on 7 November 1825 by the Earl of Liverpool, High Steward of the Borough, resident of Coombe House, Coombe Hill, and Prime Minister for fifteen years. The bridge was opened on 17 July 1828 by the Duchess of Clarence, later Queen Adelaide.

Powers to reimpose tolls were obtained for Kingston by Act of Parliament in 1825. This was a backward step for the town's trade. The charges—in force for forty-two years—were as follows:

Every person on foot . . . $\frac{1}{2}d$.
Every person with a wheelbarrow or suchlike carriage . . . $1d$.
Every horse, mule or ass, laden or unladen and not drawing . . . $1\frac{1}{2}d$.
Every horse or beast of draught drawing singly any coach, chaise, calash, chariot, gig, whiskey, chair, caravan or suchlike carriage . . . $3d$.
Every one, two or more horses or beasts of draught drawing any coach, etc. . . . $3d$.
For every additional horse or beast of draught drawing any car or any suchlike two-wheeled carriage . . . $1\frac{1}{2}d$. . . . and so on.
Every bull, ox, cow or calf . . . $\frac{1}{2}d$.
Every sheep, cow or pig per score . . . $5d$.

With the repeal of these charges, trade was unfettered. By 1870, the bridge was being used by some 25,000 people and 3,000 carriages weekly as well as by droves of sheep and cattle coming to Kingston market.

As part of Kingston's rejoicings on Freedom Day, a salute of cannon was fired as the Lord Mayor of London, accompanied by the Sheriffs, approached the bridge. A 40 ft ceremonial arch, painted to resemble bathstone, spanned the bridge roadway. Above the arch was a banner proclaiming "Free for Ever," flanked by the Union Jack and a galaxy of flags and civic crests.

Clarence Street

Clarence Street in the 1900s had the appearance of a country market town. The churchyard of All Saints was surrounded by shoulder-high spiked railings mounted on the present wall. Tombstones still marked the actual sites of graves. One of the curiosities of the street was a stuffed "mermaid" in the window of a taxidermist shop kept by Bill Parslow at No. 10.

The great success story of Clarence Street and, indeed, of

Kingston, is the rise of Bentalls store. The book *A Merchant Adventurer* by Charles Herbert tells the saga of the House of Bentall under the strong guidance of Mr Leonard Hugh Bentall, son of Mr Frank Bentall, the firm's founder. The proceeds of this book's sale went to Kington's Steadfast Sea Cadet Corps.

The present chairman and joint managing director is Mr Rowan Bentall, grandson of Frank Bentall. His book *My Store of Memories,* a deserved bestseller, continues the firm's history in lively style until 1974.

One of the important business premises in Clarence Street in the 1900s was the gunsmith and ironmongery shop at No. 39. It belonged to Thomas Goldring, whose duties included caring for the guns and the famous wrought iron gates at Hampton Court Palace.

London Road

London Road in the 1900s had several claims to fame. This was the principal highway into Kingston from London, joining Clarence Street, in those days, at the junction with Eden Street. Here were the royal grammar school, many pubs—and a place to pawn pianos. The pawnbrokers was Harry Sprunt's at the corner of London Road and Cambridge Road. He advertised "Money advanced; plate, watches, jewellery, clocks, bronzes, china, furniture, cycles, pianofortes."

The Lovekyn Chapel, London Road, spans the years and its history led directly to the establishment of the Queen Elizabeth Grammar School (Kingston Grammar School). It is at the junction of Queen Elizabeth Road with London Road. Dedicated to St. Mary Magdalen in 1309, it is a direct link with the early middle ages. Edward Lovekyn, born in Kingston, became a wealthy London merchant. He and his brother Robert endowed the chapel with land to maintain a chaplain to hold divine service there daily for his family and all faithful people deceased. After confiscation under King Henry VIII's dissolution of the monasteries, Queen Elizabeth I endowed the building as a school.

One of the great businesses of the London Road was Smithers & Sons, at Nos. 104–14 in 1902. They were carmen, contractors, warehousemen, house furnishers and carpet beaters. They built up a large removal and depository trade as well as extending the furnishing side. "Vic Smithers was a very close personal friend of the Emms family," said Sammy Emms. "His firm fitted out some two hundred of my cabin cruisers and house boats during the time I had my 'Boats and Cars' premises off Kingston High Street.

"The development of Thames Street, Clarence Street and Eden Street killed off London Road as a trading centre except for car sales firms. I had hoped to build a greyhound racing stadium where the

Norbiton Hall flats now stand, at the junction of London Road and Cambridge Road. Prosperity would have come to that end of the town so far as traders were concerned if that plan had gone through. There was a public inquiry but the Ministry turned the scheme down owing to parking difficulties."

Colourful characters seem to have abounded in London Road at the turn of the century. Garratt, the bootmaker at No. 35, had a son who claimed to be the world top heavyweight swimmer. He used to swim with weights piled on his back. He was an exceptionally strong man and was engaged to demonstrate his ability in London.

Most exciting of all was the annual visit of Sequire, the cure-all man who specialised in rheumatic diseases. His arrival in the town would be heralded by a triumphant parade with decorated boats on lorries and all manner of floats. His "pitch" was a tent in a field near Densham's Laundry, London Road. The treatment he offered consisted of rubbing on a certain ointment. This was performed by helpers in the tent, while a brass band played to drown the yells of those whose stiffened limbs found the massage painful. Sequire's visit was the event of the year for many people.

Those were the days of horses, carriages and carts, "fly-masters" and livery stables. Possibly the best-known of these in London Road was James Sumner's premises at No. 186, billed as the Jolly Sailors Livery Stables. He hired out waggonettes and all manner of horse-drawn vehicles as well as riding horses.

Two remarkable—and historic—premises still in use in London Road are a "garage-like" building near today's C. & A. stores at the present junction of London Road and Clarence Street, and the early Victorian "double cottages", known in 1902 as Manor House West and Manor House East, almost opposite St Peter's Church, Norbiton.

The "garage-like" building in 1902 was the Kingston, Surbiton and District Fire Brigade headquarters. The Manor House cottages with their elaborate balustraded roof and chimney turrets are built on or very near the site of Archbishop Tillotson's palace which later became an overflow classroom for Kingston Grammar School (then in Lovekyn Chapel) and later served as Kingston's workhouse.

Around the 1900s the site of today's massive C. & A. clothing store was the Main Motor Cycle Works. By 1902, three shops—a fruiterer's, an upholsterer's and a nurseryman's premises—had replaced the motor cycle works. Later a noted Kingston character, Punch Shepherd, had a cafe there, famous for its $\frac{1}{4}d$. breakfasts for schoolchildren, hungry when their parents went early to work.

Betty Pie's Alley, now Hawks Passage by today's Kingston Grammar School, was originally named after an old lady who kept a little shop there. It was famed for gingerbread and mulberry pies. In the summer, old Betty served teas under a fine mulberry tree in her garden.

Wood Street

All trace of a once highly-important street has vanished. The address of Kingston railway station today is Wood Street. In the 1900s, although the station was on the same site, the address was No. 1 Ceres Road, an area devoted to nursery gardens (possibly the origin of the street's name).

Wood Street begins on the Market Place side of Clarence Street, and joins Church Street opposite the Kingston War Memorial. Today, the street goes right through to join Richmond Road at Kingston railway station, but originally, Wood Street finished at its junction with Lower Ham Road; the continuation up to Kingston railway station was Ceres Road.

In the 1900s a number of premises occupied Bentalls' present site. In Wood Street stood two schools belonging to Kingston Parish Church. They were All Saints National School (boys and girls), built in 1873, and All Saints Infants School (1881), which together could accommodate 750 children. The average attendance was about 500 pupils. Next to the schools was All Saints Mission House. Further down the street was All Saints Vicarage, now built into the fabric of Bentalls' Wood Street premises. A pub—the Red Lion—also occupied part of the original site, with "beer retailer" Martin Williams as licensee. On the opposite side of Wood Street, the most notable building was Kingston Corporation Baths, opened on 18 October 1897 by the Mayor, Mr Alfred W. Homersham, after whom Homersham Road, Kingston, is named. The establishment consisted of a swimming bath, 90 ft by 30 ft, constructed so that it could be used as a hall in winter. There were also five first-class and six second-class slipper baths for women and six first class and ten second-class men's slipper baths.

In 1900 the superintendent was Mr Gerald O'Rouke; he was succeeded in 1908 by Mr Danny Emms (Sammy's brother), a man whose record is never likely to be exceeded: when he retired in 1950, it was reckoned that he had personally taught 20,000 people to swim. He was more at home in the water than out of it, and at the age of twelve, he won a bar of chocolate—and a spanking—from his father for diving into the Thames from Kingston bridge. One of Danny's best remembered feats was his Kingston regatta speciality when he used to dive into the water through a flaming hoop.

In the 1900s the Water Lane to Lower Ham Road area, now mainly occupied by Bentalls' multi-storey car park, was occupied by Down Hall, a mansion with lawns that stretched down to the Thames.

The Steadfast Sea Cadet Corps premises by the Thames now occupies part of this land. There is a story that on the lawns of the Down Hall mansion, stood a stone statue which represented Queen Anne, placed there by one of the Queen's ladies-in-waiting, thought to have lived at Down Hall. Today, the only memory of the house is Down Hall Road, by Kingston railway bridge over Lower Ham Road.

Kingston's almost desperate wish to have a railway station in the centre of the town was gratified on 1 July 1863.

Through lack of foresight, Kingston city fathers had originally refused to allow trains to come to Kingston for fear of losing the valuable coaching trade. The success of the "New Kingston" station, opened in what is now Surbiton in 1838, reversed their opinion. River-trade, a vital part of Kingston commerce, had almost vanished into train-trade; Kingston wanted it back.

Thus the town's first railway station was opened in 1863. It was not, as today, connected to London via Malden and Wimbledon. It was an extension of the line to London via Richmond. Only by near-pleading had Kingston city fathers managed to lure the railway constructors across the Thames to central Kingston. The first scheme was to have Hampton Wick as the termination of Kingston's London line.

Thames Side: Steadfast Sea Cadets

The Steadfast Sea Cadet headquarters, Thames Side, has a remarkable history. The corps' name came from the brigantine *Steadfast,* bought for £200 in 1911 and moored off Queen's Promenade, Surbiton. Its role, created by volunteers, was to provide a training ship for local lads. It was converted for sea cadet use at a cost of £400. The ship was familiarly known as "The Brig"; today the Steadfast Corps officers have carried on the tradition by calling their headquarters "The Brig".

By 1913, seventy-two boys had applied to join the Corps. Although not a "nursery" for the Royal Navy, boys interested in seafaring were encouraged to enrol. They all underwent training on the brig *Steadfast,* piping aboard many distinguished visitors including the Duchess of Albany.

The brig was an excellent training ground for youngsters, but by 1928 she was getting old and too expensive to maintain, so she was sold, fetching £110. The ship's company moved to temporary headquarters in the Volunteers Drill Hall, Orchard Road. At that time there was a volunteer staff of three (Lieut. W. J Muddock (later Lieut.-Cmdr.), Lieut. F. S. Stevens and Sub-Lieut. A. Beale) and fifty-seven cadets.

In 1934, the present headquarters site was made available by Mr Leonard Bentall, son of the store's founder, who was on the unit's formation committee and later became a trustee. Mr Valentine Knapp was the secretary of the original committee.

In 1936, the new headquarters was opened by Mr. Lloyd George. It had been built at a cost of £5,556. In 1951, extensions built as a memorial to Mr Leonard Bentall were opened by Admiral Lord Fraser of North Cape (First Sea Lord 1948-51).

The Parents and Friends Association of the Steadfast Corps has worked valiantly over the years raising money to assist in meeting running costs. The year 1970 was the Association's twenty-first anniversary, marked by a donation of £1,500 to the Corps. In the twenty-one preceding years, the Association had raised £17,664. The Corps' Silver Band, founded by Lieut. John Hodgson, who received the M.B.E. for his work done with the band, is also a fine money-raiser at summer fetes and displays. The Corps provided a Guard of Honour when King George VI and Queen Elizabeth came to Kingston to open the electricity power station at Canbury Gardens and also when Queen Elizabeth II came to Kingston at the 400th anniversary celebrations of Kingston Grammar School. Annually, the Steadfast Band and Corps attend the Remembrance Day services at Kingston War Memorial.

The commanding officer at the present time is Lieut.-Cmdr. W. T. Weir, who has grown up with the unit. He joined Steadfast as a cadet in 1942 at the age of eleven. In business life he is a Midland Bank Official.

Fife Road

Fife Road, joining Ceres Road and Clarence Street, was Kingston's theatrical and "pop" centre in the 1900s. The Royal County Theatre, Fife Road, was in its heyday and R. White's mineral water works—renowned throughout the country—was where part of the back of Bentalls is now. The Royal County Theatre was opened on 9 October 1897. The site had previously been the Albany Hall, used for concerts. The theatre held an audience of 1,250, and presented first-class touring companies and an annual pantomime. When the larger Empire Theatre was opened in Clarence Street in 1910, audiences at the Royal County Theatre declined, although the Empire was devoted, in the main, to twice-nightly variety shows.

In 1912, Fife Road theatre was converted into a "super cinema." It continued showing films until it was burned down on 8 February 1940. The site remained derelict for a number of years before redevelopment. The old Royal County Theatre has, however, an imperishable claim to fame. It was the place where Sir Charles Chaplin made his first-ever public appearance on the stage. When Sir Charles came to Britain some two years ago, he was presented with a photograph of the Fife Road theatre with a dedication recalling his stage debut.

The Fife Road "pop" centre was for many years nationally extolled in a child's skipping game. There was a "bumps" rhyme to the chant of R. White's ginger beer—the skill lay in an extra big leap with the rope at the word "ginger," signifying the drink's effervescence.

A number of women were employed at the mineral water works. They used to wear coarse crash (a type of linen) aprons and clogs. During the first world war, many of them left to work at the Sopwith aviation works, then in the former roller skating rink, Canbury Park Road. (One of the processes involved in this work turned their skins yellowish. The extra money for aviation work enabled them to buy fur coats, known in 1914-18 as "munition workers overalls." Any woman in Kingston with a yellow face and a fur coat was automatically classed as an aviation worker.)

Education also had its place in the story of Fife Road. Almost opposite the County Theatre was Kingston Polytechnic, state contemporary records. It shared further education with the Technical and Arts Schools, between Kingston Hall Road and St James's Road, opened in 1899. The Poly's classes were held in the Young Men's Club and Institute, Fife Road.

The first-ever cinema in Britain to show nothing but motion pictures is also said to have been in Fife Road. A book called *The Romance of the Movies* by Leslie Woods relates that a young Kingston man called Lane and his friend purchased some American cinematographic apparatus and showed films in an empty shop in Fife Road, believed to be No. 47. The flickering films failed to attract audiences. The young men pasted paper over the windows in an attempt to darken the shop, and stood outside urging passers-by to enter. They were still unable to attract sufficient numbers—and Kingson's first real cinema vanished.

Richmond Road

An important part of Kingston's educational growth took place in Richmond Road, in what is now an annexe of Kingston College of Further Education, which was built in Richmond Road as a Kingston public school for some 680 children: boys, girls and infants. A foundation stone on a little white building, originally the Infants School, states: "This stone was laid by H.R.H. The Duchess of Clarence, 1st September, 1828." This same Duchess, later Queen Adelaide, had only some weeks earlier visited Kingston to open the new bridge across the Thames.

In those days, many of the children paid 1$d.$ a week towards the cost of their tuition. The State grant was, in effect, based on a sliding scale adjusted according to the excellence or otherwise of reports submitted annually by H.M. Inspectors.

Here is an extract taken from the *Annual Report and List of Subscribers to the Public Schools, Richmond Road* for the year 1900. Reporting on the Boys School, H.M. Inspector states: "The boys are in very good order and instruction as a rule is very creditable. Algebra and chemistry are well taught. The Drawing Inspector reports that on the whole the work is well done but that there is a want of precision in the sketching which necessitates much clearing up before a satisfactory drawing results."

As regards the Girls School, H.M. Inspector reported: "Distinct improvement has been made in the order and the tone of the school is more pleasing. Instruction is given more quietly and better methods are being employed. The syllabus is well drawn out and the term reports are full and thorough."

On the 1900 Infants School, the report is "Capital order is maintained. The instruction is well supervised and is given with much care and success. The teaching in Object Lessons merits a word of special praise."

Canbury Park Road, a turning off Richmond Road near today's Kingston railway bridge, is the birthplace of Kingston's fame as an aviation town—enshrined today in Hawker Siddeley Aviation Ltd., Richmond Road. The building which helped win the first world war was originally the premises of Kingston's renowned Roller Skating Rink. This had opened with a flourish on 23 September 1909. Among trophies which could be won at the rink was a huge silver cup for the one-mile championship race—sixteen times round the rink. Roller skating hockey matches were also favoured.

In 1912, Sopwith Aviation Company bought the premises and began using it as an aircraft factory. In the years 1915-19, it became the company's experimental shop while their main offices and works, now Kingston Polytechnic Annexe, were built further up Canbury Park Road.

In 1920, the H. G. Hawker Engineering Co. Ltd. took over both Canbury Park Road premises and the Sopwith Aviation Company's works, still in use today, at the rear of the Hawker Siddeley premises, Richmond Road, Ham.

Here in the words of one of the world's most respected aviation experts, the editor of *Jane's All the World's Aircraft*—Mr J. W. R. Taylor of Alexandra Drive, Surbiton—is the importance of Hawker's to the world.

"The name Hawker and its predecessor Sopwith have been synonymous with the world's finest single-seater combat aircraft for more than sixty years. The most successful fighter of World War One was the Sopwith Camel (1,294 victories). The mainstay of the

R.A.F. Fighter Command in the Battle of Britain was the Hawker Hurricane. The vertical take-off Hawker Siddeley Harrier of the present era is the brilliant first of a whole new kind of fighting aircraft."

Harry Hawker, an Australian, came to England in 1911 with capital of £100 and an urgent wish to fly. He joined the Sopwith Aviation Company at Brooklands in 1912. He worked fifteen hours a day, seven days a week, for £2. After competing in a number of air events, he and Kenneth Mackenzie-Grieve, flying a machine called "Sopwith Atlantic," attempted to cross the Atlantic from Newfoundland to Britain and win the Daily Mail prize for the first Atlantic air crossing. They came down in the sea but their lives were saved as they carried a small dinghy on the plane's fuselage and kept afloat until they were rescued. They were awarded £5,000 by Lord Northcliffe (Daily Mail) and the Air Force Cross for gallantry.

Harry Hawker died at the age of thirty-two while flying a Nieuport Goshawk in preparation for the Aerial Derby. He is buried in the churchyard of St Paul's, Hook.

The Sopwith Company, which flourished abundantly during the first world war, had got into financial difficulties and had been reorganised under Hawker's name. By the middle of 1920, it was obvious that, with no more orders from the Royal Air Force and enormous war-time taxes owing to the Exchequer, the Sopwith Company could no longer carry on. It was, therefore, wound up while still solvent and, in the September of that year, the H. G. Hawker Engineering Company Ltd. was brought into being with Harry Hawker, Fred Sigrist, a brilliant engineer, Bill Eyre and Tommy Sopwith as directors. The object was to create a small firm to make aircraft when the demand rose and to keep the wheels turning by building motor cycles and other "odds and ends."

By the time of Hawker's death, the company was on firmer ground with plenty of work in hand. By 1933, any pretence at general engineering had disappeared from the company's activities and the name of Hawker Aircraft was adopted.

One of the most significant steps in the company's progress was taken in 1925 when Sopwith entrusted the whole future of the new company to a thirty-one-year-old aircraft designer, Sydney Camm.

"For four decades, Sydney Camm was responsible for design work at Hawker's. His work is unmatched in the world," said Mr Taylor. "Those of us who were privileged to learn our aircraft engineering under his guidance can never repay the debt."

By 1936, the company had amalgamated with a number of manufacturers to form the Hawker Siddeley Company with a capital of six million pounds—ready and able to face the nation's call at the time of the Munich crisis. The financial expansion had already enabled the comparatively small Hawker Company to go ahead with the development of Camm's great project—the Hurricane. Nearly

15,000 Hurricanes were built. The final Hurricane, which is kept in immaculate condition, was purchased from the company by the Government in mid-1944 and is suitably inscribed "The Last of the Many." During the summer of 1968, it flew for the film "The Battle of Britain."

The Fairfield

Just as Kingston Market Place has always been the commercial "heart" of Kingston, so the Fairfield has been the town's playground. The quiet tree-lined lawns which today comprise Fairfield Recreation Ground give little hint of their lusty past. Once medieval pageants were held on the ground, and regular cock-fighting took place there. Where the Municipal Car Park is today was a village pump providing water and a place for gossip. Once hundreds watched the renowned Middle Mill Cricket Club matches. Now only a handful of spectators follow the Fairfield teams.

At one time, the Fairfield was an open space of some twenty acres. Kingston Council leased the present Fairfield as a recreation ground for the town. It had long been an open space but by the mid-1800s it was an unsafe area after dark, the haunt of the town's roughs.

In earlier days, tournaments and jousts were held there when the Gloucesters and the Warwicks were said to have occupied Kingston Castle. All through Elizabethan and Stuart times the area was used for local sports and fairs. By 1837, it had degenerated into an untidy waste but as late as 1880 Kingston's November Fair was still held there. This event attracted "thousands of people from all parts of the Kingdom and there were as many as 20,000 sheep, 10,000 head of cattle and 1,000 horses exposed for sale in a single day," state records.

It was in 1868 that the Fairfield recreation ground, as we know it today, was established, with the provision of fencing and general tidying up. With the coming of houses to nearby roads, civic pride asserted itself.

The *Kingston Corporation Act* of 1900 allowed the Council to purchase the whole of the Fairfield land.

Here the town owes a debt to that great benefactor of learning, Scottish millionaire Andrew Carnegie. He provided £8,400 for the Fairfield's Kingston Library, designed in the Georgian style of architecture, and came personally to open the building on 11 May 1903. The adjoining museum and art gallery were paid for by the Corporation and were opened by Lord Rosebery on 31 October 1904.

On opening, the library had 8,200 books for loan and a reference

Fig. 3 Kingston Market Place, with an Esher-bound horse bus.

Fig. 4 Regatta Day, Canbury Gardens.

Fig. 5 The Bandstand, Canbury Gardens. There was a similar one at Queen's Promenade, Surbiton.

Fig. 6   Seaplane testing, near Canbury Gardens.

collection of 2,000. With a vast expansion of the Kingston Central Library book stock, both in loan and in the reference collection, district and branch libraries and a mobile library now bring its facilities to all parts of the borough. There is also a domiciliary service for the housebound, and the needs of children are given special care.

One of the delights of today's Fairfield are its fine plane trees. They were planted in 1904.

In the days of Kingston's own M.C.C., as the Middle Mill Cricket Club was affectionately called by its spectators, hundreds used to watch the games, and rows of seats lined the pitch boundary. The team had its headquarters at The Cricketers, Fairfield South, as did the Kingston Town Cricket Club. The Middle Mill Football Club had its headquarters at The Albion, Fairfield Road.

The Middle Mill was on the Hogsmill River, at the end of Mill Street, a side-turning off Fairfield South. It is in Mill Street that the Kingston public house with the intriguing name "The Cocoanut" stands, rebuilt from old days. Its name derives from the days when coconut matting was made at Middle Mill. The name "Kelly's" is, however, most usually associated with the mill for it was there that the early Kelly's street directories were produced.

Directly opposite The Cricketers public house is the site of a beautiful majolica drinking fountain, erected by public subscription to mark the Diamond Jubilee of Queen Victoria. Today, a modest concrete "stump" fountain presented by the Metropolitan Drinking Fountain and Cattle Trough Association replaces the magnificent Jubilee memento. Diligent enquiries revealed that over the years the Queen Victoria fountain had become badly damaged by the weather and that it ended its days in a Corporation dump.

However, the Fairfield was the scene of much civic festivity in honour of the old Queen's 1897 Jubilee. This included a school treat for 4,000 children who assembled to receive Jubilee Medals from the Mayor, Councillor Alfred Homersham.

At the far end of the Fairfield is St Joseph's Roman Catholic Primary School, built originally as Tiffin Boys and Girls Schools, now in separate premises in London Road and in Richmond Road respectively.

The Tiffin schools owe their foundation to Kingston brothers Thomas and John Tiffin, brewers. In 1638 and 1639, they left bequests for the "benefit of children of the honest poor" of Kingston. Money from this bequest was used to purchase seventeen acres of land at West-by-Thames, today's Bittoms area. Part of the money for the Fairfield schools was raised by selling some four acres of this land. The schools were designed by Mr Loxwood King and were opened on 20 January 1880.

Many distinguished men have been headmaster, but the man who set the tone of the school in the early days was the great headmaster,

Mr Charles J. Grist, head for thirty-nine years (1880-1919). In tribute to his memory, the Tiffin Boys School Grist Playing Fields in East Molesey were opened in July 1949, by Col. C. B. Hartley, president of the Rugby Football Union.

As the Tiffin schools at the Fairfield expanded, it was necessary to find increased accommodation. The new Tiffin Girls School at St. James's Road, Kingston, was built in 1899. Miss A. J. Flavell was an outstanding headmistress in those early days. The Tiffin Boys School left the Fairfield for their present London Road premises in 1929.

"Liquid history" still runs beneath the Fairfield: it is the Coombe Springs water. The Cardinal Wolsey conduit pipes from Coombe Hill to Hampton Court Palace, still largely in place, enter the Fairfield at the junction of Minerva Road with Fairfield Road. They cross the recreation ground on their way to the Thames bank at today's Town End public gardens. Originally, some three and a half miles of leaden pipes, each 25 ft long, took water from Coombe Hill to the Palace. Cardinal Wolsey believed the water had health-giving properties.

The Coombe water suppy continued to the Palace until around 1876, when a boat fouled the pipes which, despite their shingle covering on the river bed, were at risk during times of drought. In 1894, the warrants were withdrawn which authorised the supply of royal venison to landowners under whose property pipes passed. This was a "fee" for using their subsoil as a path for the pipes. In 1900, the whole system was wound up. One of the major protestors when the royal venison permits were withdrawn was the Duke of Cambridge, from whose land on Coombe Hill the water came.

Today, the Fairfield provides an oasis of peace in central Kingston, but it was nearly the site of Kingston's first railway station within the town centre. The first plan put forward by some members of Kingston Council for the station site suggested the Fairfield. After a stormy public meeting, the present site of Kingston station was chosen—and the Fairfield was saved.

Canbury Gardens

Kingston's royal river has been for centuries a highway for kings, queens, commerce and pleasure. It has been immortalised in many books. Jerome K. Jerome's classic *Three Men in a Boat,* published in 1889, gives Kingston as the start of their hilarious river journey.

Elegance and romance, allied with a homely and "high-scented" trade, form part of Kingston's Thames-side story over the years. The Row Barge, Old Bridge Street, and The Outrigger, Thames side, are two public houses repeatedly mentioned in books on Kingston.

From King Henry VIII onwards Britain's rulers frequently travelled by state barge to and from Hampton Court to their Palace of Whitehall. Although "row barge" is an authentic name for a pulling boat, I feel the pub's name may be a corruption of "royal barge"—especially as the inn sign depicts a state barge.

Kingston railway bridge, completed in 1863, is a fine example of Victorian ironwork. Among goods transported across it in the early days was one of Kingston's most famous local products—native guano.

This was produced at the municipally-owned Kingston upon Thames Fertiliser department and sold nation-wide. Advertisements of the day state: "This manure is extensively used by agriculturists and horticulturists throughout the country and has been manufactured and supplied from the Kingston works since 1888." After extolling the value of the Kingston brand, the brochure states: "Finally, we should like to call the attention of all gardeners to the words of Rudyard Kipling: 'Our England is a garden and such gardens are not made by singing "Oh, How beautiful" and sitting in the shade.' "

The delights of this guano were manifold and assailed the nostrils of Kingstonians. For many years, the name "Perfume Parade" was given to the narrow avenue of chestnut trees which today joins Kings Road to Thames side at the end of Canbury Gardens, since for some time the guano filter beds adjoined this avenue. The space is now occupied by the power station.

The original offices of the guano works were No. 1 Down Hall Road. An early advertising brochure gives a picture of the works with their name boldly painted on the roof of a main building. A similar picture, the only discernable difference being that the words "Native Guano for All Crops" have been removed, is reproduced in the handsome souvenir booklet issued by the British Electricity Authority to mark the opening of the present Kingston Power Station by King George VI on 27 October 1948.

The new power station replaced the Kingston Corporation Electricity Works, established in October 1893, and sharing the Native Guano company's site.

Electric street lighting was introduced in Kingston on 4 November 1893, and a supply to private consumers was made available three days later. The Electricity Works was one of Britain's first municipally-owned generating stations. From 1 September 1931, as a result of a bulk supply agreement between Kingston and the London and Home Counties Joint Electricity Board, Kingston's generating station was connected with the General Electricity Board's grid system.

Canbury Gardens was created from drained land, once osier beds. They were opened on 8 November 1890, by the Mayor, Councillor John East. A picture of the ceremony shows that the fine row of plane trees now between the towpath and the gardens was not yet planted; a 1905 picture shows the trees as saplings. Were they planted as part of Kingston's Coronation celebrations to mark the crowning of King Edward VII and Queen Alexandra in 1902?

One such tree in Canbury Gardens was indeed planted on Coronation Day itself—on 9 August 1902. It was planted by Kingston's Mayor, Dr W. S. St Lawrence Finny, as proclaimed by a plaque attached to a circlet of railings around the tree (a smallish oak). It was planted well back from the river, the site being close to the present line of poplar trees masking the electricity station. The ceremonial silver spade which Dr Finny used is now part of Kingston's regalia. It was with this spade that Princess Alexandra planted a silver birch at Surbiton Lagoon in January 1977 in the symbolic presentation of twenty-five trees to Queen Elizabeth II by Kingston citizens under the Mayoral Silver Jubilee £5,000 Tree Appeal. The Mayor, Councillor Frank Steptoe and Mr Rowan Bentall, a member of the Appeal Committee, also took part in the ceremonial planting. Under the Appeal scheme, groves of trees in Her Majesty's honour are to be planted at selected sites throughout the borough.

To revert to Canbury Gardens, both there and at the Queen's Promenade, Surbiton, residents used to enjoy military band music and concert party entertainment at attractive bandstands during the summer. There were regular mid-week and weekend performances. A chalet teahouse at the Ham end of Canbury Gardens provided refreshment for many a courting couple or residents out for a stroll. This is now replaced by Kingston Corporation's fine boathouse and cafeteria, winner of architectural commendation.

After Canbury Gardens, road and towpath combine for a space, and here the curve of the river gives splendid views back to Kingston town and forward towards Teddington.

At the point when the Lower Ham Road turns inland towards Richmond Road and where the towpath alone goes on to Teddington Lock, stood a massive tree. It was hollow inside and a man could stand upright within the mighty trunk. This was beloved by courting couples in the old days, and the names of many a young Kingston sprig and his lass were scratched inside the elm. Finally, it was filled with concrete in an endeavour to preserve the trunk. Eventually it was felled.

Its replacement stands in the same place today. Around are seats, just as they used to be years ago. A plaque states: "On this site stood the Elm known locally as the 'Half-mile' tree, probably 500 years old, removed in 1951 due to its dangerous condition and replaced in 1952", so that elm was a seedling in 1451 and 107 years old when Queen Elizabeth I came to the throne in November 1558.

2. SURBITON

Surbiton, a town created by transport, was once on two famous coaching routes: to Brighton and to Portsmouth. Then, as a community, it scarcely existed. With the coming of the railway in 1838, the town developed as it is today.

Its coaching day milestones remain: symbols of the day when the horse was king of the road. One is by the Thames near the junction of Surbiton Road and the Portsmouth Road. An elegant house nearby bears the name Milestone House. Another milestone is by the wall of a garage at the junction of Ewell Road and today's Tolworth Broadway.

In the 1900s, the horse still dominated the Surbiton roads. As late as 1862 a famous coach "The Age" was running a scheduled service on the Ewell Road route through the growing town. Wealthy men vied with each other to drive the coaches in much the same way as railway enthusiasts today seek to drive privately-owned trains on specialist tracks. "The Age" was owned by a group of such men towards the end of its illustrious career.

Surbiton Improvement Commissioners

Surbiton owes its place as "Queen of the Suburbs" to a remarkable period of home rule carried out for thirty-two years by a fifteen-man body called the "Surbiton Improvement Commissioners". Their names are enshrined in a number of local roads.

Their proud badge, the Winged Lion of St Mark's couchant with its massive paws on a book, has almost been forgotten. Their work from 1855-87 turned Surbiton into a thriving community from its early position of Kingston-on-Railway, or Kingston Junction, as it was called for a time.

The chairman of the Commissioners for seventeen years was Mr C. Walpole, commemorated in Walpole Road. The name Corkran Road recalls Mr C. Corkran, one of the first fifteen appointed to create Surbiton following a public meeting at the Southampton Hotel, the largest available building. Local determination to break from Kingston was the reason for the meeting. Residents felt too little money was being spent on their area's roads, lighting and similar facilities.

The present Claremont Road—then called Railway Road—joining Kingston to what is now Surbiton railway station was in such a deplorable state that certain local residents paid for repairs out of their own pockets, and had a long fight with Kingston Council to get the money back.

This provided practically the last straw in local dissatisfaction and the *Surbiton Improvement Act* was passed by Parliament in 1855 setting up the Surbiton Improvement Commissioners.

Their rule lasted until 1887, when their last chairman was Mr T. Guilford, whose name is commemorated in the most frequently mis-spelled name in the borough—Guilford Avenue at the top of Villiers Avenue.

By the time the Improvement Commissioners' work had come to an end, Surbiton had grown to a town with a rateable value of £87,000, compared with Kingston's rateable value of £102,286 for the same year (1887).

A woman who left her mark on the area in those days—and still influences the route taken by certain buses—is Mrs John Shrubsole, a formidable lady who lived at Surbiton Hall, and a member of the family who owned Shrubsole Bank, Kingston Market Place. Her home was opposite the Surbiton Assembly Rooms. Trams taking patrons to the Assembly Rooms from Kingston were originally routed to continue up Surbiton Road and turn right towards the railway station at the Maple Road intersection, which would have brought the trams in front of Surbiton Hall. Mrs Shrubsole decreed otherwise and the tram route was switched round the back of her property, along Surbiton Crescent.

Surbiton Assembly Rooms owe their construction to a group of public-spirited Surbitonians who, in 1882, took up £1 shares to raise the sum of £6,000 needed to build the long-desired concert and meeting halls. The fine terra cotta work embellishing the facade is especially noteworthy.

Surbiton Road

At the point where the Surbiton Road former coaching route to Brighton leaves the Portsmouth Road beside the Thames, there is now a past-and-present reminder of Kingston's long military history. On the Portsmouth Road is the imposing Territorial Army and Volunteer Reserve building housing Kingston's "Medics", the 221 (Surrey) Field Ambulance R.A.M.C. (V) and a platoon of "A" Company 5th (Volunteer) Battalion, the Queen's Regiment.

In Surbiton Road is the Regimental Headquarters, Queen's Regiment (Surrey Office) and Museum. This museum is possibly the most remarkable—and least visited by the public—of all available historic records in Kingston today. It is open daily from Monday to Friday at specified hours, except on public holidays. The exhibits unfold a vivid panorama of military history from Stuart times to the present day. These include uniforms, weapons, letters from soldiers and remarkable trivia, including eight gold-tipped cigarettes, each measuring some six inches long, which once belonged to King Farouk of Egypt. These were handed to the British Intelligence Service by an Egyptian informer as proof that he had access to the Royal Palace and could thus supply information, prior to the King's forced abdication on 23 July 1952.

The exhibits were originally housed in Kingston Barracks, Kings Road, of which only the gate-house now remains, the site having been redeveloped by the War Office as married quarters.

One of the earliest exhibits is a facsimile of the 1662 wedding contract between King Charles II and Catherine of Braganza. On her marriage, the fortified town of Tangier became the property of England. This led to the formation of the Tangier Regiment of Foot, one of the ancestor regiments of today's Queen's Regiment.

Among the more recent exhibits at the museum are the drums of the 3rd and 4th Battalions of the Queen's Royal Surrey Regiment (T.A.), presented to the museum in 1968. The East Surrey's souvenirs from the last war on display include the massive brass door knocker and handle from a bank at Cassino, Italy, taken in May 1944. The regiment was fighting there as part of the 8th Army.

One of Kingston's most impressive military ceremonies in recent years was the bestowing of the Freedom of Entry on the 1st Battalion and the 6th (Territorial) Battalion, the Queen's Regiment (Queen's Surrey), at the Guildhall on 14 October 1967. The occasion was—to the day and to the hour—the 306th anniversary of the first muster parade of the regiment. Two detachments of the battalions and the band of the 1st Battalion marched from the Territorial Headquarters, Portsmouth Road, for the ceremony. After inspecting the troops at the rear of the Guildhall, the Mayor, Councillor R. P. Oliver, spoke of his pride in welcoming the Surrey battalions on their first official visit to Kingston since the reorganisation of both the Regular and Territorial Army. The Council's resolution, passed in May, was then read, conferring "the right, title, privilege, honour and distinction of marching through the Royal Borough of Kingston upon Thames on all ceremonial occasions with bayonets fixed, colours flying and bands playing."

In his speech thanking the Council, Major-General F. Piggott, Deputy Colonel, the Queen's Regiment, said, "The spirits of former comrades, gathered today over Putney Heath, where the first muster of the regiment took place, must surely, on hearing the martial music, have flown here to watch over this parade."

As a "truly remarkable birthday present" to the battalions, Major-General Piggott accepted the illuminated and framed "Right of Entry" document presented to him by the Mayor.

Portsmouth Road

As the Portsmouth Road left Kingston High Street and entered the Surbiton area, the Queen's Promenade presented a regal appearance in the 1900s. Many notables had imposing mansions along the road. The majority of these houses are now replaced by blocks of flats.

Dr Thomas Barnado, founder of the homes for children, lived (and died, in 1905) at St Leonard's Lodge, 51 Portsmouth Road. It was Dr Barnardo's presence locally which may have led to the establishment of the Barnardo Home for Boys in what is now the Blenheim Gardens area of Galsworthy Road, Kingston.

Originally, the building was the Metropolitan Convalescent Institute but, in 1892, it was purchased by the National Society for the Protection of Young Girls and was opened by their patroness, Princess Louise, Duchess of Argyll, Queen Victoria's daughter. The object was to save young girls aged from eleven to fifteen from exposure to temptation and from being abandoned. They were educated by the National Society to work as domestic servants and were placed in suitable positions, with the Society acting at all times as guardians. There were 140 girls in the Kingston home in 1899.

The Queen's Promenade itself was indeed a royal route. St. Raphael's Catholic Church, built in 1846-7 by Mr Alexander Raphael of Surbiton Place, was technically within the boundaries of the old Kingston borough. It drew a considerable congregation from Surbiton —and from Esher. It was a favourite place for weddings among the French Royalist refugees who flocked to Esher to join the Court of the exiled King Louis-Philippe of France and his queen, who settled in Claremont House, Esher, around 1848, by permission of Queen Victoria. The royal pair escaped to England under the guise of Mr and Mrs Smith, the king wearing a red wig.

When the French royal family attended Mass at St Raphael's, a Kingston Grammar School boy chosen to take part in the service had permission to be late for class. The royal coach would stop by his home and take him to the church.

In 1895, the Duchess D'Aosta presented a gold chalice to St Raphael's as a thanks offering for the blessing of the marriage of the Duke D'Aosta. During closure of the church and its allied buildings for a time in 1896, services were held for several years in St James's Hall, St James's Road, Kingston.

Surbiton's first town map was based on the Seething Wells area of the Portsmouth Road. It was completed in January 1865, taking the datum line for all levels as a bench mark cut on the Portsmouth Road boundary stone between Kingston and Thames Ditton. The map was made on orders from the Surbiton Improvement Commissioners.

Seething Wells itself, a spring of water with supposed opthalmic properties, had a chance of becoming a spa in earlier days, but the plan was abandoned. The Wells became the site of the Chelsea and Lambeth Waterworks, Portsmouth Road, later the Metropolitan Water Board and now the Thames Water Authority. The solid Victorian masonry, an excellent example of the Gothic style, forms a notable landmark. Now there are two castellated chimneys, originally there were six. Four were pulled down in the early 1930s when the works were redesigned.

The wells are recalled by the name of Seething Wells Lane, the first turning right after Brighton Road leaves the Portsmouth Road on its way to Surbiton proper.

Brighton Road

One of the oldest parts of Surbiton is Cottage Grove, a turning on the left on the way up Brighton Road towards Victoria Road, Surbiton's High Street. Originally the Grove's name was George Street. A number of Surbiton's roads seem to have changed their names between 1850 and the 1900s. Maple Road, the turning before Cottage Grove after leaving the Portsmouth Road, was originally Terry's Lane, after a wealthy merchant named Mr Christopher Terry. He built Maple Lodge, hence the final name of the road.

Commercial prosperity came to Brighton Road with the building of Electric Parade, an imposing row of shops between Balaclava Road and Victoria Avenue. Today, the shops are still there but their "electrifying" name graces the slip road at the rear of the premises instead.

A railway bridge now divides Brighton Road from Upper Brighton Road, which was once called by the former name up as far as The Maypole public house at the junction with Ditton Road.

A more spacious age is recalled by property around the five-road junction at the top of today's Upper Brighton Road. Langley Avenue, Langley Road and Langley Grove recall the wealthy Thomas Langley. It was for this man that in 1808 John Nash, architect of Marble Arch and Regent Street, built Southborough House, Ashcombe Avenue. This house is still the glory of Surbiton. For a time it was lived in by Charles Corkran, one of the Surbiton Improvement Commissioners.

On the left side of Upper Brighton Road, just prior to Langley Road, is today a large Victorian house, for many years the premises of the Surbiton section of the London Royal Eye Hospital. During the second world war, the house was taken over to escape the London blitz. A little further along the road, in 1899, flourished a successful private school, St Bernards, kept by the Misses Miller. The imposing house is still there, No. 19 Upper Brighton Road. Today it is used for the local offices of Government departments.

Victoria Road

Victoria Road forms the heart of patriotic Surbiton, created by the Victorians' proudest achievement, the railway. Originally the road extended up the present St Mark's Hill. Today it begins at Surbiton Railway station—the town's third station.

The first was a smallish house at the bottom of the deep cutting crossed by the present Ewell Road railway bridge. The nearby public house, the Railway Tavern, recalls the 1838 station, site of the official opening attended by local dignatories, although the Mayor of Kingston refused to be present. The name of this new station was "New Kingston" or "Kingston on Railway." It was reached by a precipitous flight of steps.

The site of the present Surbiton station was given to the town by Mr Thomas Pooley, the original developer of Surbiton as it is today. The shops along the Ewell Road and Brighton Road owe their existence to the old coaching route, but Victoria Road is a product of the railway.

The Coutts banking family was the saviour of Surbiton in the early days of the town's development, Coutts stepped in when Mr Pooley's finances got out of hand. He had promoted a noble scheme for the station area, but was unable to carry it through. His policy entailed building a house, selling it and using the money to pay for further building. This worked well in the initial stages, but eventually the town looked like a derelict area when viewed from the trains. Pooley's finances were taken over by Coutts, and the town was saved from disaster. Coutts' beneficience is remembered today in the present Royal Borough of Kingston's coat-of-arms. The stags which support the central shield come from the original Surbiton Borough Council coat-of-arms. They were derived from the crest of Coutts.

The £5,500 fund for building St Mark's Church in June 1845 was handsomely subscribed to by the Coutts banking family. Additionally they paid entirely for the first St Mark's vicarage, a Gothic-style mansion which until comparatively recently fronted St Mark's Hill. It is now replaced by Assheton-Bennett House.

The original St Mark's Church—for 824 worshippers—was a very different design from the present building. It was in Gothic style with a square central tower surmounted by pinnacles The architects were F. Stevens and G. Alexander. Only nine years after it was built, however, the church was radically redesigned and enlarged to accommodate 1,015 sittings, under plans prepared by Mr Philip Hardwicke. The central tower was partially removed, the roof raised and a tower with a spire was placed at the north-west corner of the church.

During the second world war, the church was very badly damaged by enemy bombing. It was eventually rebuilt and reconsecrated in 1960. A cairn of stones at the rear of Surbiton's war memorial, Ewell Road, is composed of stones from the blitzed St Mark's Church. There is a memorial plaque on the cairn.

St Andrew's Church, Maple Road, was largely paid for by Baroness Burdett-Coutts. This remarkable woman was created Baroness in 1871 by Queen Victoria. It was at that time the only instance of a peerage being bestowed upon a woman in recognition of her public achievement. She lived until 1906 and her many benefactions are part of the social history of Victorian England.

In 1881 the Baroness married Mr William Ashmead Bartlett, the son of an Englishman who had emigrated to the United States. He was, at the time of the marriage, twenty-eight and she was sixty-seven. He had become her principal assistant in her manifold acts of benevolence.

To return to Victoria Road: it was here that Surbiton's first Cottage Hospital stood, opened in October 1870, at York Villa, the site of the present Surbiton main post office. The present post office was built in 1898. An earlier post office was in shop premises almost opposite today's railway station.

The Cottage Hospital was moved to a site which had been purchased in St James's Road. This became Claremont Hospital, later part of the Kingston and Long Grove Hospital Group and finally of the Kingston and Richmond Area Health Authority. It was closed in late 1976.

The foundation stone of the Claremont Hospital was laid by Archdeacon Burney, vicar of St Mark's, in 1882. It was opened for patients the following year, costing in all £5,000 for the site, building and equipment. As the town grew, the hospital became inadequate and the present Surbiton Hospital, Ewell Road, was opened by the Duchess of Gloucester on 28 July 1936.

With the coming of the steam railway, residents feared that sparks from the engines would cause fires. Thus Surbiton's second fire station was established. The first, in Firebell Alley, Ewell Road, was for the higher end of the town. At the end of this alley can still be seen a small huddle of buildings which housed the fire station. They were rented for this purpose at £10 a year in 1865 from a Mr Walter. A firebell was erected on the roof, and in 1870 another bell was placed in Surbiton railway station yard. (Surbiton's first fire engine was purchased in 1863. It was a Roberts' patent manual engine costing £52. The engine, named "The Talbot", was kept for the first two years in the offices of the Surbiton Improvement Commissioners, forerunners of Surbiton Urban District Council.) The Victoria Road area was provided with a fire station at the rear of Mudies, the builders, then almost exactly opposite today's post office.

Also at Mudies was the first premises of the Surbiton Club, founded in 1873. Their present club in St James's Road is built on a site purchased in 1898 for £1,500. The twelve members of the club's committee issued 100 debentures at £50 each, carrying an interest of four per cent, to cover the cost of the new premises.

The Surbiton Constitution Club, St Mark's Hill, was established at a later date in a Victorian mansion, modernised and extended. The first president was Sir George Penny, M.P. for Kingston.

A focal point of the Surbiton station complex is today, as seventy-five years ago, the Claremont Road Coronation Clock Tower. It commemorates the crowning of King Edward VII in 1902.

The erection of the clock tower got off to a shaky start. A public subscription was organised by Dr Coleman, the District Medical Officer. Three sites were chosen—Claremont Road, Victoria Recreation Ground and a second Claremont Road position. Surrey County Council objected to the first Claremont Road site for traffic reasons. Eventually, the present site was decided upon. The scaffolding went up in 1905 and came down in 1908.

Surbiton Hill

Surbiton may have been paid for by bankers, but it was "purified" by teetotallers. Much of its sewage disposal system was paid for by loans from the United Kingdom Temperance Institution. This body owned considerable land in the Surbiton Hill area, including "Teetotal Cottages" in Alpha Road, as it was then.

The Alpha Road area was the heart of old Surbiton. The name Alpha was bestowed by the Surbiton Improvement Commissioners. It was the first road they set in order after breaking from Kingston by Act of Parliament. Previously this road had been called Green Lane or Middle Lane. It was a quagmire of mud with no proper sanitation.

In the mid-1800s Surbiton's drainage in general was pitiful. A contemporary record mentions "drains going into an open ditch which runs the whole length of the road . . . stagnant sewage . . . open cesspools close to houses . . . water unfit for drinking purposes."

In 1859, things took a turn for the better. The Improvement Commissioners appointed Mr Robert Brown as Surveyor, and he undertook a sewage disposal scheme which transformed much of the district. Later, under surveyor Mr Charles Mather, further extensive improvements were undertaken.

The United Kingdom Temperance Institution lent just over half the money needed for sewerage works completed in 1884 and for clearing mortgages on earlier works.

Just as the Alpha Road area was the first Surbiton site to be transformed by the activities of the Surbiton Improvement Commissioners, today's Alpha Road estate has been reconstructed and brought up to modern housing standards by the present authorities, Kingston Borough Council.

In the old days, there was a village atmosphere of home industries: No. 2 Alpha Road was the home of John Balls, wheelwright; at No. 5 was Mrs Mary Ann Pratt, straw hat maker; No. 6 was Miss Emma Dean, lace cleaner. What visions of Victorian finery in the mansions forming the Oak Hill, Surbiton Hill and Portsmouth Road area are conveyed by the term "lace cleaner". Those were the days when everyone who was anyone had a cook, a maid, and if possible, a private carriage. Today a residents association seeks to foster a social atmosphere in the Alpha area.

Among businesses which have vanished over the years are a row of cottages in Britannia Road, each of which seems to have housed home laundries. Britannia Forge, in the hands of the Hutchings family since 1880, transferred to Mill Place Kingston, in 1973 when the Alpha area Council redevelopment was reaching its concluding stages. Prior to the 1880s a Mr John C. Aspin, a "veterinary smithy," had owned the forge. Of later years Mr Ernest Hutchings, inventor as well as blacksmith, made gates, grilles, lanterns, weathervanes and similar wrought-iron work at the forge. He retired to Berstead, near Bognor, when the move to Kingston came, leaving the forge in the hands of Mr Alfred Brown, his son-in-law.

Inhabitants of this part of upper Surbiton in general worshipped at Christ Church, King Charles Road, built in 1863 to accommodate 780. It was enlarged in 1864, in 1866 and finally in 1871, giving a total of 1,204 sittings.

The nearby Fishponds, now a public park, is a world of its own. The estate was purchased for £10,000 in May 1935 by Surbiton Urban District Council from Miss Mabel Butler and Mr Frederick Butler, members of the tobacco family. A condition of sale was that they and Miss Susannah Butler were to remain in leasehold residence for life in the house and its twelve acres of land. Today the house is let to tenants of Kingston Council.

Originally there were seven ponds on the estate. Today there is one. Fish are gone, but ducks abound. Hollyfield Road was constructed soon after the purchase of the estate, and was named after the home of Frederick Butler on Surbiton Hill.

The name is perpetuated in Hollyfield School, originally in the present King Charles Centre, Hollyfield Road. The school now occupies the Surbiton Hill premises of the former Surbiton County Grammar School for Boys. This school was transferred to Weston Green Road, Thames Ditton, and is now Surrey County Council's sixth-form Esher College.

Today's Hollyfield School is also the home of the main Surbiton Adult Education Centre. In 1970 Hollyfield pupils investigated the history of the fine Victorian mansion which is one of the school's main buildings. It was called Albury House and was built in 1856 by Mr William Edward Dunnage, one of the fifteen Surbiton Improvement Commissioners for the year 1855, the year of their establishment. It was adapted for use as a school in 1926.

History is in the road names as well as in the buildings of this part of Kingston borough. A royal escape provides one name. On 11 November 1647, King Charles I fled from Cromwellian captivity in Hampton Court Palace. He is supposed to have escaped from the rear of the Palace, fled across the Home Park, taken a boat across the Thames, and made for high ground on the "Surbiton" bank. Three horses were waiting and legend suggests that he rode off towards the coast from what is today King Charles Road, Surbiton. Villiers Road, Villiers Avenue and Villiers Path commemorate the Cavaliers' clash with Roundheads in the closing stages of the Civil War. Among the slain was Sir Francis Villiers, a youth of "surpassing beauty". He was killed at the foot of an oak which stood until comparatively recently in Villiers Path, according to colloquial history.

Berrylands

High life in Edwardian upper Surbiton was closely linked with London, and later with the cinema. Regent Road, Surbiton, is a reminder of that era.

A colourful character, Daniel Nicols, a bankrupt French wine-merchant who fled from Paris to escape his creditors, was responsible for the saga. Daniel and his wife, Celestine, were practically penniless when they reached London. They had two assets: Daniel's knowledge of wines and Celestine's ability to sew. After several modest beginnings, they purchased a tailor's shop at No. 68 Regent Street, London, and converted it into the famous Café Royal. Daniel's cellar and Celestine's care for neatness soon made the restaurant famous. The Nicols prospered accordingly. French debts of a quarter of a million pounds were paid off, naturalisation papers were taken out and the Nicols decided to find a country place to establish themselves firmly in society. They were recommended to try Surbiton—so handy for town by train. They did, and they liked the pleasant countryside and the deer (part of Surbiton Hill area was a deer park at that time).

The Nicols bought the piece of land between what is now Park Road, Berrylands, Regent Road and Surbiton Hill Park. Here they built an imposing mansion called Regent House. Part of this property is today known as Regent Cottage, Berrylands.

The de Nicols' guests (for "de" had now been added to the name), included Adelina Patti, the opera star, George Edwardes, founder of the Gaiety Theatre, and Sir Blundell Maple, creator of the furniture store. In fact, the brightest and best of the clients who frequented the

Café Royal were lavishly entertained—pink champagne was the usual drink.

The film era of this part of Surbiton centred on Vine House, then No. 8 Park Road. It was the Stoll Picture Studios, and in the mid-1920s it became Regent Studios, making educational films. Later, during the second world war, it was the Surbiton headquarters of the Surrey Territorial and Auxiliary Forces Association.

Ewell Road

Another link with Regency times in this area is Regency Cottage, Ewell Road, near the Public Library. In early days, it was called Horner Cottage. The next house, once The Sheaves, is now called Kingston House, home of Mr Sammy Emms, for over fifty years President of the Kingstonian Football Club. Today's name honours the Club. The former name recalled the famous windmill which was once on the site of Surbiton Hospital, almost opposite.

The red bricks of Kingston House and near neighbours are thought to have been made at brickfields in the Fishponds area or at a site which is now "The Wood", an idyllic park by Oakhill Grove, laid out by Surbiton Borough Corporation at a cost of £2,500 as outlined in their 1951-2 budget. The upper section of The Wood is a bird sanctuary bearing the name "Jefferies Wood." This was created following a suggestion from Mr Hockley Clarke, author, and founder in 1954 of the Surbiton and District Bird Watching Society. Richard Jefferies, a famous Edwardian journalist-naturalist, moved from Swindon, his birthplace, to Tolworth about a hundred years ago. He lived in Tolworth for five of the most productive years of his short life, as I learned from Mr Cyril F. Wright of Chickerell Road, Swindon, Secretary of the Richard Jefferies Society, founded in 1960.

Originally The Wood formed part of the garden of The Gables, now Hillcroft College for Women, South Bank. It was in the garden that the private theatre, called Gables Theatre, was built in the 1880s, originally as a "folly" for the house owner, I understand. However, it became beloved by amateur theatrical companies. In the 1920s it was flourishing. It was here that Robert Cedric Sherriff, author of *Journey's End*, the greatest of all 1914 war plays, learned his craft.

He was a member of the Kingston Rowing Club, then established on Raven's Ait. Their funds were depleted. To raise money, Sherriff undertook to write plays. They were successfully produced at the Gables Theatre by the Kingston Adventurers Dramatic Society.

The theatre seated about 250 people and until 1927 was gaslit. Soon afterwards, it was equipped with electricity and renamed Hillcroft Theatre. Around 1932, a professional repertory company were in residence until the theatre's demolition prior to the building of

Glenbuck Road flats, not long before the last war.

Hillcroft College's establishment in Surbiton, in The Gables, is a romance in itself. The fine house which had belonged to Mr Wilberforce Bryant, a member of the "match" family, was up for sale—with no purchasers. The embryo Hillcroft College, badly needing more accommodation, was then at Beckenham. It came to Surbiton in 1926 and took the name Hillcroft, celebrating the golden jubilee of its foundation in June 1970.

Mr. Thomas Wall, son of the founder of the ice-cream and sausage firm, was a lifelong friend of the college and its treasurer for many years. His generosity backed the purchase of The Gables which, as Hillcroft College, became one of the most important long-term residential adult colleges in the country. Even today, Hillcroft College receives a generous annual grant from the Thomas Wall Trust.

Chance led to Surbiton as the choice for the college's new home.

Miss Margaret Joyce Powell, one of the college lecturers, had been appointed Surrey County Librarian. She made a daily journey to County Hall, Penrhyn Road. A wait on Surbiton Station led her to walk into a nearby estate agents to ask for a mansion with at least thirty to forty bedrooms and a large garden. When the agent had recovered from the shock, he suggested The Gables, which had just come on to the market. The purchase price asked was £14,000. Mr Thomas Wall counselled offering £10,000, and the sale went through.

Practically opposite The Gables' grounds, in fact the last house before South Bank joined Glenbuck Road, was South Bank Lodge, from the 1880s to 1912 the home of one of the greatest railway engineers Britain has ever known.

He was an Ayrshire man, Dugald Drummond, one of the world's outstanding locomotive designers. For many years he was Chief Mechanical Engineer of the London and South Western Railway (Surbiton's line). Son of a permanent way inspector on the North British Railway, he received his grounding in Scotland and in Australia before coming south and taking up residence in Surbiton. Engine design and management of men were his talents.

The largest passenger locomotives in the British Isles in 1905 were designed by Drummond. They had coupled wheels 6 ft in diameter. A full account of his great work is detailed in the *History of the London and South Western Railway*.

His death at the age of seventy-two was a blow to the locomotive engineering world. He died following an operation for a scald on the leg received when inspecting an engine. Today, his house—and his trains—are no more.

Oakhill itself is a maze of twists and turns. I know the area well, and yet still manage to become confused when I drive up Oakhill

Fig. 7 Queen Victoria's Jubilee Fountain, now vanished.

Fig. 8   Raven's Ait, Surbiton, in earlier days.

Fig. 9 The Electric Parade and its magnificent clock, Brighton Road, Surbiton.

Fig. 10   St. Mark's Church, Surbiton, as first designed.

Grove. My attention is diverted by the beauty of the bird sanctuary trees on the left at the top of the hill, and I forget the twists and turns needed to achieve Ewell Road.

Some of the remaining mansions on Oakhill are splendid examples of Victorian–Edwardian domestic architecture at its best. A number are excellently preserved. In 1899 the major roads in the area were Oakhill, Oakhill Grove and Oakhill Road. (There was no mention of Oakhill Crescent; I feel this was part of Oakhill Road, which had two openings on to Ewell Road at the turn of the century.) Incidentally, "Oakhill" was two separate words in those days. In 1899 there were comparatively few houses in the area, and almost all were named.

Berrylands Farm, the last farm in the central Surbiton area, was the survivor of two almost adjacent farms: Berrylands Farm and Berry Lodge Farm. In the 1880s, Mrs Charlotte Aspin held one and Mr William White the other. Berrylands Road was then a muddy lane and the district bore the appearance of a common with furze growing on part of it.

Berry Lodge Farm was the first to go. Berrylands Farm fell under the auctioneer's hammer in July 1930. Among the "goods" sold were a dairy herd of fifty-four, including cows named Creamer, Fillpail, Lemon, Violet, Cherry, Cowslip and Crumple.

Tolworth Fountain

Where Ewell Road today meets Ditton Road and Ellerton Road, by Surbiton Police Station, is the site of the vanished Tolworth Fountain. (Incidentally, Surbiton Police Station is built at a distance from the centre of Surbiton proper because, in the early days, it was felt "not quite nice" to have a police station too close. Surbitonians considered their "Queen of the Suburbs" pride.)

The fountain was disposed of forty-one years ago, swept aside by the demands of modern traffic. Today, only one of its horse troughs remains. This is at the rear of the triangular public garden between Ditton Road and Ellerton Road.

Two pieces of the missing fountain were discovered when council workmen were preparing a hard-standing for gypsy caravans off the Kingston by-pass between Fullers Way North and Cranborne Avenue. Two pieces of the huge base and two polished granite inscribed tablets were unearthed.

One tablet read: "This drinking fountain and two plots of land were given by Mr Stephen Kavanagh of Tolworth in exchange for Old Tolworth Pond." The other tablet read: "This fountain was opened for public use by Mr G. M. Walker, J.P., Chairman of the Surbiton Urban District Council, 29th July, 1901. S. Mather,

A.M.I.C.E. Engineer and Surveyor."

The story of the fountain's dedication makes almost pathetic reading when one remembers that it was within living memory. At least a century of life, if not immortality, was anticipated on that opening day.

Five hundred schoolchildren marched in procession from St Matthew's School, Surbiton, behind the Surbiton brass band. Mr Kavanagh was highly praised for providing a hygienic alternative supply of water for cattle, horses or sheep to the Tolworth Pond, by then stagnant and half full of rubbish. Drinking cups were provided for men, women and children and there was a special trough for dogs.

A poem called "The Spirit of the Pond" was recited. A rather unfortunate line, viewed in retrospect, concluded the six-verse poem: "My granite robes will last—endure I may, while generations pass and dynasties decay."

After the formal proceedings, the five hundred schoolchildren were entertained to a hearty tea followed by a Punch and Judy show and sports. Some 150 guests were also entertained. In the early evening a large crowd gathered at the fountain to see Mrs Kavanagh pull a chain and thus light the 1,000 candlepower lamp which surmounted the fountain. After singing the National Anthem, the crowds dispersed.

By 1936, the fountain, despite the attractions of the four elegant eagles supporting the lamp standard, had become a traffic menace. The original gas jet light had been replaced by a three-lamp electric fitting. But it was doomed.

The Dittons

The removal of the former Surbiton County Grammar School to Thames Ditton, through a change of education authority following the formation of the Greater London Council, lends point to my including some Thames Ditton and Long Ditton history in this survey. Many prominent Kingston professional and business people live in the Dittons. The area's successful fight to remain a village arouses admiration.

Were the original names Thames Ditch-Town and Long Ditch-Town, or Thames Dyke-Town and Long Dyke Town? Experts differ. The Rythe, which rises in the Arbrook Common area, Esher, and enters the Thames near Winter's Bridge, Portsmouth Road, is thought to have been the "ditch" of ancient times. On the other hand, the nameboard outside St Mary's Parish Church, Long Ditton, records the following: "The Parish of Long Ditton is a very ancient one. A church has stood on this Hill of Ditton since Saxon times. The name 'Ditton' may perhaps be derived from the Dykes along the Thames."

Admittedly, the Thames has a curve at this point, but have any traces of dykes been found?

As for the Winter's Bridge area, here again there is a concealed name. Originally it was Window's Bridge, after a blacksmith named Window who erected the bridge over the Rythe watersplash of those times, largely for the benefit of his customers. Years have provided a corruption of the name.

Links with the past abound in the Dittons. These include a tomb which recalls a tragic romance, a Domesday estate where London's police horses are now trained, historic almshouses and a riverside mansion that has become a Home of Compassion.

Thames Ditton served as an "off-duty" retreat for courtiers from Hampton Court Palace across the Thames. It was a pleasant row across stream. This select social atmosphere has continued down the years.

Boyle Farm, now the Home of Compassion, High Street, was built in 1786 for a wealthy widow who lived a gay social life. Her husband, the Hon. Captain Robert Boyle Walsingham, had been drowned in 1780 when he was lost with his crew of six hundred men when the *Thunderer,* a man-of-war with seventy-four guns, foundered on a return voyage to England from the West Indies.

Always the scene of entertaining, the peak of Boyle Farm's glory was, perhaps, reached in 1827 when the "Dandies Fete" was held in the grounds. This cost £2,500, a very large sum in those days, and was paid for by the Lords de Ros, Alvanley, Castlereagh, Chesterfield and Grosvenor. Gondolas floated on the Thames and Italian opera singers entertained five hundred guests feasting in the grounds. (Later Lord de Ros, who had been born at Boyle Farm, was utterly disgraced having been found guilty of cheating at cards over a considerable period.)

The present red-brick facade of Boyle Farm was added by Mr Herbert Robertson, who bought the estate in 1890 at an auction. He sold much of the land for building plots, but the house and immediate grounds were purchased in 1903 by the Church of England Community of the Compassion of Jesus.

The building was established as a Home of Compassion and the chapel was built in 1925. Today, it is administered by the Charity Commissioners under a board of trustees. It is a nursing home for fifty old people and is supported by voluntary contributions.

Thames Ditton's tragic tombstone is in the churchyard of St Nicholas, the parish church. It is to the right of the rear of the church and bears part of a tombstone brought from Paris after partial destruction by a German shell in the Siege of Paris, 1870. A marble tablet under the Paris fragment reads: "Lady Edward Fitzgerald's remains were removed from Paris by J. P. Leonard Esq., and interred here the 21st August, 1880, by her grandchildren. The above stone was on her tomb in Montmartre cemetery and was broken by the bursting of a shell during the siege of 1870." The French stone reads: "Pamela, Ladye Edward Fitzgerald par son ami le plus devoue. LL."

As a young woman, Lady Fitzgerald, daughter of the Duke of Orleans, was one of the beauties of the Court of King Louis XVI. Her father was guillotined in the French Revolution and her husband was shot by the English in 1798 as a result of conspiring to bring arms and ammunition from the Continent to Ireland.

A central feature of the attractive Thames Ditton village is, today, the one-time drinking fountain and cattle troughs which now form a traffic roundabout. An electric light now graces the top of the fountain while plants fill the basin and troughs. The fountain was presented "to the Parish of Thames Ditton by Hannibal Speer, Esq., Lord of the Manor, A.D. 1879: Freely Given—Gratefully Accepted," states an inscription on the base. The troughs were provided by the Metropolitan Drinking Fountain and Cattle Trough Association.

The link between Imber Court (now the Metropolitan Police Mounted Branch Headquarters) and Thames Ditton's "Bridges Almshouses" in Station Road is interesting. The almshouses, six little dwellings, were established in 1720 by Henry Bridges, owner of Ember Court, now known as Imber Court.

Long Ditton, as its name signifies, progresses more or less in a straggling line from the Winter's Bridge area of the Portsmouth Road to the top of Ditton Hill.

There is a national centre for education near the parish church of St Mary at the top of Ditton Hill. This is the Woodstock Residential College of the National Union of General and Municipal Workers.

The present St Mary's Church was built in 1880. The Garden of Rest behind the church is on the site of the original Saxon church of Long Ditton. Donations for repairs to the former St Mary's Church include £100 from Oliver Cromwell himself, towards roof repairs.

In former days, one of the earliest gunpowder "factories" in Britain was situated in the Long Ditton area.

Hook

In the 1900s, the territory after The Maypole public house in Upper Brighton Road was in the hamlet of Hook, described in 1899 as "anciently La Hoke, a hamlet and ecclesiastical parish formed in 1839 out of Kingston civil parish." Today, the Kingston by-pass bisects the area.

Two principal landowners of the 1890s were Lord Foley, owner of Barwell Court, and the Earl of Lovelace, whose name is recalled in Surbiton's Lovelace Road and Lovelace Gardens.

A feature of the Hook Road (the extension of Upper Brighton

Road approaching the Kingston by-pass) is the milestone on the pavement just before the junction of Herne Road with Hook Road.

In the old days, the road, now a busy thoroughfare, was a route for farm carts going to Kingston market with their produce and with flocks of sheep and cattle being driven along the road past flowering hedgerows. It was not until the railway came to Surbiton in 1838 (with trains at first running only between Nine Elms and Woking Common) that rural conditions began to fade.

Hook had an independent village life until comparatively recently. It was an agricultural area famous for orchards, strawberry fields and farm produce.

The present parish church of St Paul, costing £3,500, was consecrated on St Paul's Day, 25 January 1883. It replaced a smaller church erected in 1838. Hook War Memorial is erected at the former gateway to the first little church. Nearby is the memorial cross to Harry George Hawker, who gave his name to the Hawker Aviation Company, ancestor of today's Hawker Siddeley Aviation Ltd. Harry Hawker and his family lived in Hook, almost opposite the church.

The present Hook church was designed by the great Victorian architect John Pollard Seddon (1827-1906). The church was entirely his creation—including the magnificent Torquay marble font and splendid stained-glass east window depicting the life of St Paul. Thomas and Eleanor Hare of the now-vanished Gosbury Hall gave the font and the window. One of the angels in the window is a portrait of their only child, Mary Eleanor Hare, who died at the age of twelve. Gosbury Hall was near the present Gosbury Hill, a Hook road.

Education in the early days in Hook was largely in the hands of church authorities. The St Paul's National School was built in 1860 for 60 children. It was enlarged in 1872 for 141 boys and girls and further enlarged in 1890 for 225 children.

Chessington

Chessington, Hook's near neighbour, is a remarkable area in Kingston borough. It has possessed seven names and at least six noble homes, and has one of the finest zoos in the country.

The names, with their approximate dates of use, are: Cisendene and Cisendune (eleventh century), Chissendon (twelfth century), Chesinden (thirteenth century), Chessingdon (fourteenth century), Chyssyndon (fifteenth century), and today, Chessington.

The notable houses are Barwell Court and Burnt Stub (the zoo), both still with us although neither are the original homes. Now vanished are Chessington Hall, Chessington Court, Gosbury Hall and Copt Gilders Hall.

The area is rich in history and in personalities.

The original Barwell Manor is believed to have belonged to Merton Priory in the early sixteenth century. In 1538, the manor, with the rest of the priory's possessions, was surrendered to the Crown when Henry VIII quarrelled with the Pope over his divorce from Catherine of Aragon and seized all Catholic church lands.

Today's Barwell Court was flourishing in 1872 when a bill of sale described it as "a delightful freehold residential property, placed in ornamental and tastefully disposed pleasure grounds containing very extensive succession houses, approached through park-like pastures studded with noble forest timber, by a carriage drive" and "having a very elevated ridge known as Winey Hill." (This ridge now belongs to Kingston Corporation, having been purchased by Surbiton Urban District Council in the early 1930s). A "nut walk" and a fish pond with "carp, tench, dace, etc." were among the attractions of Barwell Court in 1872.

Burnt Stub, today the headquarters of Chessington Zoo, had a similar exciting history. The original house was built in 1348. It became a Cavalier stronghold in the Civil War and was burnt to the ground after a siege by Cromwell's forces. Rebuilt after the Restoration, it was renamed Burnt Stub, and has continued to be known by this name. In 1919, the mansion suffered severe damage from fire but was immediately restored. Points of interest include the fourteenth century Italian overmantel in the lounge hall.

In 1919, Chessington was still very much a rural village with its own parish council. It was in that year that the late Sir Francis Barker, then Lord of the Manor, provided facilities for the reformed Chessington Cricket Club, whose forerunner flourished from the 1880s to 1909 on a ground known as Stag's Meadow, now the Cheshire Gardens area, Chessington. The land he provided is now known as the Sir Francis Barker Recreation Ground. In 1934, an area of some twenty acres was acquired by Surbiton Urban District Council from the Barker Trust, including the present recreation ground.

The Saker Pavilion, costing £4,000 and opened early in 1964 by Mr Nigel Fisher, M.P. (knighted in 1974), was named in honour of Mr Walter Saker. Mr Saker and his wife Cissie were mainstays of the cricket club for many years. He was a founder-member in 1919.

Busy, bustling Chessington, today home to thousands, was not long ago a quiet retreat linked with the arts.

Constable, whose landscapes are a glory in the world's paintings, was a close friend of a local family—the Claytons. The Claytons lived at Haycroft, a house they had built in Hook village. The house name is now recalled in Haycroft Road, off Hook Road. The family name is perpetuated in Clayton Road and also in Clayton House, a home for elderly people in Sugden Road, Long Ditton. When John Clayton died in 1866, and his wife Emily in 1879, two sons built St Matthew's Parochial School House, Surbiton, in their memory.

Fanny Burney, the eighteenth century novelist, danced with joy round two mulberry trees in the garden of now-vanished Chessington Hall. She was expressing her delight on learning, in 1778, that her first novel, the celebrated *Evelina,* was to be published.

Today the link with literature is preserved in the associations of a house in this area with the imprint of Arthur Barker, the publishing firm founded by the son of Sir Francis Barker (whose name is perpetuated by the Sir Francis Barker Ground, Leatherhead Road, Chessington). This is the half-timbered house on the right proceeding up Garrison Lane from Chessington South railway station. It was built by the late Mr Arthur Barker, and called "Whiteoaks" in commemoration of his association with the Whiteoaks series of internationally best-selling books by Mazo de la Roche. For a time the publisher lived there with his family, I learn from his son Councillor Mark Barker, a member of Kingston Borough Council, but today Whiteoaks has been turned into two flats.

Later the Barker family lived at Chessington Hall where Mark and his brothers frequently climbed Fanny Burney's mulberry trees. In the garden there was a mound on which, it is believed, once stood the summerhouse where Fanny Burney, while a guest at Chessington Hall, wrote part of her second novel *Cecilia,* the memoirs of an heiress. This book was published in 1782.

For part of the 1930s Prince Vladimir Galitzine and his family, Czarist refugees from Russia, lived at Chessington Hall. At about the same time, Doris and Anna Zinkeisen, the artists, lived at the Home Farm. Many of their renowned pictures of horses were painted at that Chessington farm. It was Anna Zinkeisen who painted the mural decorations on the liners *Queen Mary* and *Queen Elizabeth.* The sisters' work is in many public art galleries.

In 1934, the two principal land owners in the Chessington area were Merton College, Oxford, and Lady Barker.

Chessington Hall was pulled down when the present housing estate in the Garrison Lane area was built. Great dreams of progress were envisaged when Garrison Lane replaced a muddy footpath or track which led from the Leatherhead Road to the church of St Mary the Virgin on the hill top.

In 1939, the railway line from London was extended to Chessington South via Chessington North, Tolworth, Malden Manor via Motspur Park station and Raynes Park from London. Construction as far as Leatherhead and to the "stockbroker belt" was planned. The scheme foundered with the outbreak of the second world war. It was never started again.

Before abandonment, the railway line had proceeded from Chessington South under Garrison Lane and on over a bridge across

Chalky Lane, opposite Chessington Zoo. Evidence can still be seen of the now-vanished lines used by men building the chalky embankment. It continues on the Leatherhead side of Chalky Lane. Today some half-buried pieces of railway sleepers and a rusted rail "chair" or two are all that remains. The bridge over Chalky Lane was taken down some years ago as being unsafe. The tons of chalky soil forming the embankment are a mute monument to past toil.

At the top of Garrison Lane is the church of St Mary the Virgin. This church is remarkable for a number of things: its tiny size, its flint walls, its wooden steeple, its long connection with St John the Baptist, Old Malden—and its remarkable system of bellringing.

The bells of St Mary's are a tribute to a remarkable man, the Rev. William Chetwynd Stapylton, who combined work at St John the Baptist, Old Malden, and ministry at St Mary's Church and at St Mary's Mission Church, Malden Rushett. His energy was phenomenal. He literally rescued St John the Baptist and St Mary's from decay in both the physical and spiritual senses, as the church buildings were deplorable when he took up his posts in 1850. His ministry lasted forty-four years. During this time, he raised over £12,393 (a very large sum in those days) for enlarging, repairing and adorning the two churches of Malden and Chessington, their schools and the vicarage. A major restoration of Chessington Church was made in 1854.

By his work and personality, the Rev. Chetwynd Stapylton secured the respect and love of all who knew him. This is evidenced by the inscription beside St Mary's unique "belfry"—a small cupboard in which ropes for the peal of eight bells are encased. The bells are rung by pulling forward the ropes, which are secured to a tie-bar. The inscription beside this little cupboard, which is behind a small red curtain, reads: "To the Glory of God and to grateful remembrance of the 44 years earnest ministry of the Rev. Canon Chetwynd Stapylton, M.A., this peal of eight bells is placed in the tower by the parishioners and friends at the parish, 1894 A.D." A second tablet by the bell-case states that they were restored in December 1967, through donations of parishioners and a legacy from Winifred Judson, formerly of Chessington, who died on 7 December 1966.

The Bonesgate Stream, a tributary of the Hogsmill River, today passes under the road at the place where Moor Lane, Chessington, becomes Chessington Road, West Ewell. The winding and narrow watercourse forms the section of Kingston borough boundary from Moor Lane to Kingston Road, the dual carriageway connecting Tolworth with Ewell. Until comparatively recently, there was a watersplash at the Bonesgate junction between Moor Lane and Chessington Road. An Automobile Association depth indicator informed motorists about the state of the 'splash at all times.

The name Bonesgate has a sombre derivation according to local belief. Bones of victims from the outbreaks of plague in London were buried there, it is thought.

Life was hard for working people in the 1900s. Several years ago, I heard from the late Mrs Annie Muir then living in Sydney, Australia. She had worked on the land at Chessington as a young woman, when she was Annie Ford.

In strawberry picking time, Annie rose at 3.30 a.m. and was paid 2d. a punnet in the early part of the season. Later when the strawberries were plentiful, they were picked by the peck, worth 6d. to 8d. a time. Her daily wage for general market garden work was 1s. 6d. Sometimes, she would pick blackberries from the hedgerows and take them to the Kingston jam factory, pushing them there in an old pram.

Rents, too, were different. Annie paid 5s. a week for her Chessington cottage. She married a Scotsman during the first world war and emigrated to Australia when peace came.

Leaving the Bonesgate area and proceeding towards the Tolworth underpass and roundabout on the Kingston by-pass, the most fascinating historical feature *en route* is "Old Kingston Road" (the present Kingston Borough Central Parks Nursery is off this road); this was superseded by today's dual carriageway from Tolworth to Ewell and now only a tiny section remains, but to me this is part of an old royal route. It is the direct route from Henry VIII's magnificent Nonsuch Palace, one of the wonders of Europe, to Hampton Court Palace, which Cardinal Wolsey found expedient to present to his master.

Despite Henry's preference for Hampton Court, Nonsuch was a favourite residence of Queen Elizabeth I. Some years ago, her banqueting hall was rediscovered. Charles II doomed the palace when he gave it to his favourite Barbara Villiers, as she later sold it piecemeal to pay debts.

Malden Rushett

The last community of Kingston borough on the route to Leatherhead is Malden Rushett. A benefice of Merton College, Oxford, the parish was once intimately connected with Malden, and was designated Malden-cum-Chessington coming under the ecclesiastical care of St John the Baptist Church, Old Malden, until 1938, when Chessington was released from the Malden parish and transferred as an independent parish to the Diocese of Guildford. Its churches were St John the Baptist, Old Malden, and St Mary the Virgin, Chessington, in effect a "daughter" church.

An early mission church, established in the 1850s, used to provide the Malden Rushett area with services. It was opened by the redoubtable Rev. Chetwynd Stapylton, of St John the Baptist, Old Malden. He used to walk fifteen miles there and back from Old Malden to take services at the little church, clearly marked on the 1898 map of the area. (This map may be consulted at Kingston Central Library, Reference Department, as may similar items of local interest.)

Today, right on the Surbiton boundary (since 1965 the Royal Borough's boundary) is one of the most interesting road features in the area. It is a Corporation of London boundary post in the forecourt of The Star public house. (It also marks the boundary of "V" Division, Metropolitan Police, headquarters Kingston Police Station.) The post is exactly twenty miles from the old General Post Office in the City of London, and dates from the days when duty was levied by the City Corporation on coal and wine entering London. This tax was first levied in 1666 for rebuilding the City after the Great Fire and was subsequently devoted to metropolitan improvements. The City's debt was cleared in 1834 and the duties were abolished in 1899. A number of these posts, bearing the City of London coat-of-arms, can be seen at points marking the twenty-mile boundary. Old maps show posts at all major entrances to London.

Malden Rushett's first school, established in 1822, was a lean-to shed beside the Star. The shed still exists, but a new school was built in 1863.

Another route out of central Kingston passes along Villiers Road and Villiers Avenue. Originally, Villiers Avenue was a tree-lined track called Clay Lane, after clay which was found there and used at the local brickworks. Villiers Road was called Oil Mill Lane until around 1924 when the present bridge over the Hogsmill was built. Until then, a narrow plank bridge served pedestrians. Carts, carriages or motor-cars used the watersplash. Villiers Avenue remained Clay Lane until after the wooden bridge had been replaced and building development took place towards the Rising Sun public house at the top of today's Villiers Avenue. The original Rising Sun was the "headquarters" of the Irish labourers employed to construct the Surbiton railway cutting and the embankment leading to Malden.

The name Oil Mill Lane was derived from an oil mill on the site of Kingston Corporation's present Highways Department, off Villiers Road. This was bought around 1895 by a Mr William Smith who had inherited his father's candlemaking and soap works. Mr Smith's "Volvolutum" soap, incidentally, was famed throughout Britain for its efficient cleansing powers and gentle properties. Part of his factory premises is still in use and nearby Oil Mill House, now Council property, lends a Regency appearance to this very twentieth century area.

In its heyday, the South Western Sanitary Laundry stood on the opposite side of Oil Mill Lane. This laundry, of which the site is now part of the Vine Products huge plant, gave employment to many local girls and women at a time when domestic service was the only alternative for most school leavers. The laundry was originally established in 1872 as Kingston Steam Laundry, with much advertised open-air drying grounds.

Nearer to Kingston along Villiers Road is Bonner Hill Girls Secondary School. Originally Bonner Hill School was for infants, and for boys and girls up to the age of thirteen, but soon after the school was opened the school-leaving age was raised to fourteen. The foundation stone of Bonner Hill School was laid in 1905. At the outset, some children paid a charge of 1d. a week towards the cost of their lessons. Today, only girls are taught at the school. When the present school was erected, it was a showplace for Kingston and Surrey County Council's education system. It cost £21,000 to build and was on a two-acre site purchased from Kingston Grammar School for £2,500.

Norbiton

Hawks Road, which joins Villiers Road to today's Cambridge Road, a main thoroughfare from Kingston to Malden, has an interesting history. At one time, it was the centre of Kingston's Italian colony, a number of whom were organ grinders.

Originally the route along Cambridge Road and up to Malden was known as "The Wanderings", according to old maps. This road was not properly made up until the coming of the United Tramways service following the introduction of trams into Kingston in 1906.

Cambridge Road's name is a tribute to H.R.H. Adolphus Frederick, Duke of Cambridge, son of George III. It was in his memory that the Cambridge Asylum for Widows of N.C.O.s and Privates of Her Majesty's Land Forces was founded in 1851. This home was—until destroyed in the last war—on the site of the present Cambridge Gardens flats. The original lodge, with its royal Cambridge Home cypher, can still be seen at the entrance to today's flats. The ground on which the home was built was given by Adolphus' son, Field Marshal H.R.H. George, Duke of Cambridge. The foundation stone was laid by the Prince Consort, Prince Albert, on 19 June 1852.

In 1944 devastation caused by enemy bombing in the middle of the night of 22 February caused the Home's evacuation. Two of the widows in residence were killed when the main structure received a direct hit. Arrangements were immediately made by the W.V.S. to move the remaining widows to two empty houses on Kingston Hill. Later, two Victorian mansions at East Molesey were purchased. These, joined together, form the present attractive Home with splendid grounds. These houses are Courtlands and Hurst Lodge, Hurst Park Road.

The Home is a sister home to the Royal Hospital, Chelsea, whose pensioners each Easter and Christmas bring a complete party to the widows with food, drinks, entertainment and even washers-up.

In the 1850's Norbiton Common isolated the Malden area from Kingston proper. The Common stretched across the present Mount Pleasant housing estate to what is now Coombe Road, Coombe Lane West and beyond.

Two great buildings were built on the Kingston fringe of Norbiton Common. They were The Union or Institute and the Metropolitan Convalescent Institute. The latter became Princess Louise's Home for Girls, which, in turn, became Dr Barnardo's Home for Boys, now the site of Blenheim Gardens, Galsworthy Road.

The Union has been transformed into the imposing Kingston Hospital. When it was first erected, in 1839, The Union was known to local people as the "Palace of the Poor." Previously Kingston's workhouse had been in temporary accommodation in cramped quarters opposite St Peter's Church, Norbiton. Earlier, it had shared a debtors prison in Heathen Street (later called Eden Street).

The new "palace" cost £10,500 and could house seven hundred men and women in what was considered excellent accommodation. Its gatehouse can still be seen opposite Norbiton railway station. Some of the buildings remain in Kingston Hospital's premises, to be replaced as soon as financial conditions permit.

Children were not inmates of The Union. They were given a home some way off in what is now the Roselands Clinic and Health Department buildings on Kingston Road, New Malden, just before the railway bridge. A glance at the cottage-style buildings there will recall the cottage homes of many Dr Barnardo settlements.

The present site of the Springfield Hospital annexe on this route— just prior to the junction of Beresford Road with Kingston Road— was Kingston Union's former extensive farm and farm buildings, and the formidable brick walls fronting Kingston Road here today probably date from that era. They look remarkably "institutional." The Springfield Hospital, incidentally, is part of Springfield Psychiatric Hospital, Beechcroft Road, Tooting.

3. MALDEN AND COOMBE

Kingston Road

After Kingston Road railway bridge, prior to 1906, there was little of interest beside the rutted road on its way to New Malden. Contemporary photographs, however, show several Victorian stately villas, almost mansions compared with the workers' cottages of the day. Of these, Mecklenburg House, next to Malden Branch Library, is the most interesting.

Before the present library was purpose-built and opened in March 1941, Malden's library was in Mecklenburg House. The service was part of the Surrey County Library system until the creation of the Greater London Council in 1965 when the library, instead of being shared between Malden and Coombe Borough Council and Surrey, became Kingston Borough Council's responsibility.

Prior to being in Mecklenburg House, the Malden–Surrey library had been established in a little brick "hut" in the grounds of nearby Park Farm, Park Road. Park Farm has become the site of Park Court flats.

Mecklenburg House has a royal derivation for its name. It recalls the fact that the largest landowners in the area, the Dukes of Cambridge, father and son, were related to the German Duke of Mecklenburg-Strelitz through marriage. In 1843, Princess Augusta, daughter of Adolphus, Duke of Cambridge, married the Grand Duke's son and heir.

Today, Mecklenburg House is a well-preserved veteran of public service. After passing out of private hands, it became in turn a convent, Malden's library and the Rates Department of the former Borough of Malden and Coombe.

The convent was short-lived. This was born of the dream of a man who made Malden an important Catholic religious and education centre. The man was Father Eugene O'Sullivan, parish priest of St Joseph's, Malden, for over forty-five years, until his death. He was succeeded by Father Hugh Hunt, later Monsignor Hugh Hunt.

Father O'Sullivan founded St Joseph's, the church now on the opposite side of the road to Mecklenburg House. He began services in 1905 for a congregation of thirty in a house called "Inglenook". This house stood on the site of the present St. Joseph's sanctuary. The work prospered, and at the time of the church's diamond jubilee, in 1965, over two thousand were attending masses regularly, and the congregations have increased still further.

Early in the century, Father O'Sullivan invited a company of Sisters of the Nativity to come to Malden from Sittingbourne, Kent, and to found a religious community in Mecklenburg House. The nuns (not a teaching order) found insufficient support and left the area.

Father O'Sullivan, undaunted by the nuns' lack of success, repeatedly appealed to the Mother Provincial of the Order of the Holy Cross, a teaching order, to come to Malden and found a school. This they did in 1931, and the present Holy Cross Convent School, Sandal Road, was established in a Victorian house, still standing amid much expansion. The motto *Ecce domus quam sibi condendam curavit Johannes* is carved above the doorway. It means "This is the house that Jack built". Like the nursery rhyme, the school has gone on growing. The Holy Cross Convent itself is now in a specially built complex in Lynton Road. It was opened in 1969.

Between Malden Branch Library and the Fountain roundabout by Malden Police Station are a number of solid late Victorian houses. These have seen first the trams, then omnibuses, next trolley-buses and now diesel buses on this major Kingston–Malden route.

The Fountain roundabout's name dates from the horse-and-cart era. There was once a real drinking fountain for men and beast on the site. It was a splendid gift to the growing town from the local branch of the Band of Mercy. The opening ceremony took place in 1894, attended by a decorated cart, whose horse, no doubt, took the first official drink. The fountain was twice knocked down—and was removed after the second disaster in June 1932, when a furniture van collided with it. The first disaster occurred when overhanging wood on a cart broke the lamp-carrying central spire of the fountain as the horses turned away having finished drinking.

Graham Spicer Institute

One of the oldest and most successful community service centres in Kingston borough has its headquarters in a former "rebel" church in New Malden High Street. It is the Graham Spicer Institute, founded as a Bible class, run by trustees of the Graham Spicer Foundation, and the Graham Spicer Club, concerned with the membership's activities of football, cricket and table tennis.

Two men's dreams culminated in the creation of today's centre. They were Mr F. Somner Merryweather, a founding father of New Malden, and Mr Graham Prockter Spicer, a director of the paper manufacturing company. Mr Merryweather, I understand, was connected with the Merryweather fire-fighting appliances firm which is still in business in South London. Mr Merryweather and his family lived in Sandal Road, Malden (their house was on the site of Berkeley Court). Mr Spicer lived in the now-demolished "Voewood," Motspur Park, hence today's Voewood Close on that site.

It was the early endeavours of Mr Merryweather which provided a haven for Mr Spicer's Bible class at a later date. The story goes back to the days when New Malden had no church of its own and was part of the administrative as well as the spiritual organisation of Kingston.

Mr Merryweather became chairman of the Malden and Coombe Local Board in 1867, a year after the reorganisation of local government had set up Local Boards and the Malden and Coombe area was divorced from Kingston. He remained chairman until 1875 and subsequently became chairman of the Maldens and Coombe Urban District Council, under a further reorganisation from 1894-1900.

Mr Merryweather assisted in the establishment of New Malden's first church, the little St James's Church in Poplar Walk. This church flourished and, following a gift of land from the Duke of Cambridge, the present Christ Church, Coombe Road, was built in 1865 to accommodate the larger congregation.

However, in 1870, a breakaway group of dissenters calling themselves "members of the Free Church of England" erected an iron structure on what is the present site of the Graham Spicer Institute. The rear portion of this building was used as the meeting place of the Malden and Coombe Local Board—in effect, it was the growing community's first "Council Offices". The land was given, I understand, by Mr Merryweather. He later returned to the "fold" of Christ Church.

The Free Church building was known as the Church of the Holy Trinity. It drew sufficient support to warrant a more permanent building, and in 1882 the iron structure was sold and the present stone building erected. Incidentally, the iron church was re-erected by its purchaser as an electricity sub-station in East Molesey.

After some years, support for the Holy Trinity Church dwindled and the stone building was offered for sale. It was purchased by Mr Graham Spicer for his Bible class. The growth of this class and its influence locally is part of the emergence of New Malden.

It was originally founded by a Mr G. Hurst in 1900 as Christ Church Bible Class. Mr Graham Spicer took charge in 1905. In 1910, Mr Spicer installed the class in a room above a shop owned by Mr W. Pearce, forerunner of Mr Tudor Williams, founder of the present High Street store. After several moves, Mr Spicer brought his class back to Tudor Williams' premises, then established. He ran the Bible class in conjunction with Dr Hugh Cran, a local doctor.

Early activities of the Institute–Bible-class included rambling, cricket and football, and at least one visit to the Continent.

The first Graham Spicer Football ground was adjacent to the

former Holy Trinity Church. It was on the site of today's Malden Adult Education Centre (formerly Malden and Coombe Borough Offices) and of Malden's present fire station.

During the first world war, a number of Graham Spicer lads were killed in action. Mr Spicer used to travel all over the country visiting Malden men in the Forces and used to meet as many of his lads as possible at the railway stations and ports on their return to "Blighty" from the front.

Perhaps as a result of overtaxing his strength, Mr Spicer succumbed, as did many others, in the appalling post-war influenza epidemic.

Mr Spicer had been personally responsible for providing finance to run the Bible class, and his generosity was further shown in his will which left the buildings to the Institute together with money in endowment for its upkeep. His friend, Dr Cran, was nominated as the first President and he named the foundation the Graham Spicer Institute.

From 1918 to 1939, the Institute was the "life and soul of the village," recalls Mr Wilfred Wiles, member for many years of the Graham Spicer Club and chairman of Malden and Coombe Civic Society. "After the war, with youth clubs springing up everywhere, support declined. Males only, compulsory Bible class attendance and no alcohol on the premises were factors in the fall of support," he explained. "The Institute had been recognised by the Charity Commissioners in 1922 and in 1949 its football team amalgamated with another club to form the Malden Town Football Club, although the Institute continued to play in its own name in the Kingston and Wimbledon District Leagues. In the late 1940s women were admitted to club membership in the badminton and table tennis sections."

In the past few years, progress in the table tennis section has been especially remarkable with across-the-board successes in both the senior and junior sections.

Central Malden

In the days of New Malden's emergence as a community, the term "plucky little Malden" was applied to the area because its inhabitants had fought a plan by far-larger Richmond to create a sewage farm for that town's waste on what is now the Blagdon Road civic complex.

The centre of the town, once Coombe Road, then called Malden Road and now the High Street, was always called "the village" in the old days, and is still referred to by that name by older inhabitants.

An excellent train service and the two fifteen-storey skyscrapers, built in 1965–6, adjoining the railway station have prevented the town's

Fig. 11 Tolworth's lost fountain—its remains were found buried.

Fig. 12 King Edward VII's Coronation Clocktower, Surbiton.

Fig. 13   Ewell Road, Surbiton, before 1905.

Fig. 14   The Bonesgate public house, Chessington, in early days. Note the two seated policemen, the swinging Bonesgate sign and the watersplash.

shopping centre from degenerating into an off-shoot of Kingston. A daily influx of employees has provided the shops with ample customers for a quick turnover of produce and goods.

New Malden's birth and growth were entirely due to the coming of the railway. The station was opened on 1 December 1846—eight years after the opening of Surbiton station and seventeen years before Kingston achieved a railway station. The line between Kingston and Malden, in fact, was not opened until 1 January 1869. This was because Kingston was originally connected to London only via Hampton Wick and Richmond. Even when the Kingston line did come to Malden, its route to London was circuitous. It went from Malden to Wimbledon and then on via Tooting and Herne Hill to Ludgate Hill station, near what later became Holborn Viaduct station. The original name for the New Malden railway station was "Coombe for Malden"; later it became "Malden for Coombe." The Coombe tag was not dropped until after 1935.

Prior to the coming of the railway, Malden was considered to be a marshy swamp. Grafton Road, leading off today's Malden High Street and backing on to the railway, was originally laid out as Providence Place, some said because the help of Providence was needed to negotiate the perpetual winter flooding along that road.

Their Royal Highnesses, the Dukes of Cambridge, father and son, Adolphus (1774–1850) and George (1819–1904) were the most important landowners in the Coombe area. Merton College, Oxford, owned much of New Malden and Old Malden.

King Edward VII was a frequent visitor to houses on Coombe Hill, and Lily Langtry lived for a time at a house in Kingston Vale.

All in all, New Malden was a very loyal town, according to the names of roads leading off the High Street, which reflect these aristocratic connections—with practically only one exception: Blagdon Road, the first turning right off Malden High Street proceeding from the Fountain roundabout towards the railway station. Blagdon Road is named after Blagdon Farm, once in the area. The next road towards the station is Kings Avenue, then Dukes Avenue and on the opposite side of the High Street, proceeding back to the roundabout, there is Grafton Road, after the Duke of Grafton, and Cambridge Road, after their Royal Highnesses.

Civic pride came hard on commercial growth in New Malden and the "Town Hall" of the Maldens (then plural in name) and Coombe Urban District Council (the present building of Malden Adult Education Centre) was erected in 1905. Until this time, since its formation under the *District Councils Act* of 1895, the Maldens and Coombe body had met in premises at the rear of the Holy Trinity Church, later the Graham Spicer Institute.

The Council's coat-of-arms—a beehive, signifying industry—can still be seen carved above the main entrance. When the town, then called Malden and Coombe, was granted borough status in 1936, the crest was changed. The new crest can be seen on the balcony of Malden Branch Library, Kingston Road, but it disappeared from official use in 1965 when Kingston, Surbiton and Malden and Coombe were amalgamated into the present Royal Borough of Kingston upon Thames, under the creation of the Greater London Council.

The Malden borough motto was *Ducit amor oppidi*—"the love of our town leads us." Heraldic symbols include a stag representing Richmond Park, with a ducal crown round its neck recalling the Dukes of Cambridge; the bay leaf on which the stag rests signifies Roman remains found locally. On the shield, a cross on a green chevron represents Maeldune (the Cross on the Hill)—the former name of Old Malden. This section has an ermine field to indicate Coombe's long connection with royalty. The bands above and below the cross are taken from the arms of Merton College, Oxford.

Today's Royal Borough of Kingston's coat-of-arms has Malden's stag and the Malden shield at the top, Surbiton's stags at the sides and in the centre are the three salmon of the ancient Kingston arms.

Next to today's Malden Adult Education Centre (former Council Offices) is the town's fire station, now operated by the Greater London Council. This building has hardly changed since it was first erected. Originally the appliances were horse-drawn—the same horses being used to pull the town's dust carts when not on fire duty. The horses were kept in stables at the rear. The only visible structural alteration since the change from horse to motor appliances is that the front of the station has been built out to accommodate the bonnets of the present fire engines. When the doors are open, it is possible to see the inner arches of ornamental brickwork which were once the front facade.

The town's first fire station was at No. 1 Acacia Grove, the home of Mr A. E. Coles, Fly Proprietor. He drove the horse-drawn fire engine when necessary and kept 1,000 ft of hose at his home.

All firemen were volunteers in those days. Originally, two call-boys were employed to round up a crew to take out an appliance. When the fire station was built next to the Council Offices, a maroon summoned the men—usually dustmen. If out on their rounds, they would unharness their horses and ride them back to the fire station.

A good-hearted social life permeated New Malden. The firemen's annual fete was a treat appreciated by all and the town band was the pride of all local citizens.

Nevertheless, the Law needed a dignified home, and £500—the biggest price ever paid locally for a plot of land at that time—was spent on purchasing the site of the present police station, a building unchanged in external appearance since it was first erected.

Incidentally, the Fountain Hotel was known originally as the Norbiton Park Hotel. It was renamed in deference to the public's desire to call the area after the town's proudest acquisition, the drinking fountain in the centre of the crossroads.

Although during its history New Malden has had three cinemas, today none remains. These were a little cinema in Coombe Road, just past the railway station (today, a chemist shop), the New Malden Picture Theatre (later called The Plaza) at the corner of the then Malden Road (now the High Street) and Sussex Road, and finally the magnificent Odeon at Shannon's Corner, Burlington Road. All are gone. The Plaza was burned down on 27 December 1936. The site lay derelict for a number of years, but it is now the Royal Arsenal Co-Operative Stores furniture and household goods department store.

New Malden's Churches

Further down Malden's main highway, opposite the present Malden Adult Education Centre, is the modern Malden Methodist church, built in 1932 on the site of the 1867 church. Extensive Sunday school and church hall accommodation is at the rear of the church. A £3,000 refurbishment scheme for redecoration was put in hand prior to the 1967 centenary celebrations.

Money from sweets and drapery gave Malden one of her finest churches—the present United Reformed Church, Malden Road, originally the Congregational Church.

Before the turn of the century, property developers laid out a fine housing estate in the Burlington Road area, and the need was felt for a non-conformist church in addition to the Wesleyan Chapel built in 1867. That chapel, enlarged and rebuilt, is the present Methodist Church, Malden High Street.

The birth of the new non-conformist church was on 20 April 1881. On that date, a group of eighteen men and women signed a covenant, a copy of which hangs in today's United Reformed Church at the junction of Cavendish Road and Malden Road, just past the Fountain Hotel.

The covenant states: "We whose names are hereunto subscribed do hereby unite ourselves together as a Christian Church in the Presence of God and, by the assistance of His Holy Spirit, give up ourselves first to the Lord and then to each other in the Lord, humbly praying that we may be built up a Spiritual House to offer up spiritual sacrifices acceptable to God by Jesus Christ. (Signed) Charles Woodroffe, Caroline S. Heather, Sarah S. Woodroffe, Christina F. Derry, Charles Derry, Emily K. Derry, Christina Derry, Clara E. Derry, James Pascall, Ada L. Derry, Elizabeth S. Pascall, Arthur D. Derry, Charles G. Woodroffe, Alfred E. Derry, Maud E. Woodroffe, Adeline P. Woodroffe, Frederick Heather, Mary E. Love."

In all, two Pascalls and eight Derrys, sweet manufacturers and

London drapers, are on the list. Mary E. Love, the only name not "family" on the list, was a housekeeper. The families lived in the Westbury Road area and, during the church-building, services were held in their homes.

Behind the church, which is still as when it was built, are several useful halls. On the inner wall of the main hall is a plaque stating: "This Stone was laid on 13th January, 1881, by John King, the donor of the ground on which these buildings stand."

Mr King was a prominent local builder. Old maps show that a pond once existed near the land. Fortunately the church and halls subsoil is firm, but the manse which once fronted Malden Road, next to the church, subsided and was demolished some years ago. A lawn, now in its place, provides a site for outdoor activities.

The years from 1860 to 1900 were a period of great church- and chapel-building in this area as in the rest of England. St Paul's Church, Kingston Hill, celebrated its centenary in June 1976. St Matthew's Church, Surbiton, commemorated its hundredth anniversary in 1975. St John the Baptist Church, Old Malden, commemorated the hundredth anniversary of enlargement with special events from April to December 1975.

In New Malden, besides the building of Christ Church (consecrated December 1866), the Wesleyan chapel (1867) and the Congregational Church (1881), a Christ Church Mission Room was founded in Kingston Road, almost half-way between New Malden and Kingston, in 1885. This corrugated iron building, now rebuilt as the church of St John the Divine, was built as the result of a ten-day mission at Christ Church.

The building of the present church of St John the Divine, daughter to Christ Church, took place in 1939, with the dedication service on 7 January 1940.

Meanwhile, church development had been taking place at the other end of Christ Church parish. This was the building of St James's Mission Church on a site in Burlington Road now occupied by a capacious office building. The name of the little mission church, and of today's St James's Church, Malden Road, recalls the original name of New Malden's first Church; the temporary church called St James's, built to accommodate eighty people, in Poplar Walk (now Poplar Grove) which was New Malden's first Anglican church. The building of Christ Church, in 1866-7, on land given by Prince George, Duke of Cambridge, resulted in the loss of the name St James. The name was revived when the attractive little mission church was built in 1903 (at a cost of £1,025).

In 1929, the parish of Christ Church was split into two areas to form the parishes of Christ Church and St James. The fine new St James's Church, Malden Road, was built in 1932-3.

With the coming of the new church, the mission church became

St James's Parish Hall and later was used to provide overflow classrooms for Burlington Road schools. When, in the mid-1940s, a number of polio cases occurred among New Malden children, some thought, for a time, that unsuitable accommodation at St James's Hall might have been a contributory factor.

The present St James's Church Hall, Malden Road, was built from the proceeds of the sale of the old mission church.

The nearby Burlington schools came shortly after the church development in that area. The infants and junior schools were built in 1906 with the secondary girls schools built in 1908. The girls school pupils were transferred to Coombe Girls School not long ago.

Pupils at the Burlington schools in the mid-1940s to the 1950s had a perfect adventure playground behind the old St James's Mission Hall. It was the Blagdon Road pottery "quarry". After school, boys used to catch newts and frogs in the shallow pond at the base of the huge pit, then near the present site of Brycbox. All Malden will remember the huge pottery chimney which towered over the area. Many will remember the excitement when it was demolished by being blown up.

Few know, however, that the Blagdon Potteries made a small fortune in the 1920s out of the extension of the London Underground system towards Morden. They agreed to allow tons of the London clay excavated during the tunnelling to be brought to Malden and dumped on the pottery's land. It was delivered free—and then the pottery owners found that it was excellent for making bricks.

Towards Old Malden

Going on towards Old Malden from the St James's Church area, those who lived locally before the last war will recall the gracious Woodfield Hotel, now replaced by Woodfield House, the large block of flats on the left side of the junction of Blake's Lane and Malden Road. During the second world war, this hotel was a home for people bombed out of their Malden homes. It was commandeered by the Malden and Coombe Borough Council for that purpose. Woodfield Gardens, on the opposite side of the by-pass, also recalls its name.

Blake's Lane and Blake's Avenue both commemorate the name of Squire Blake on whose land Beverley School now stands. He was a dominating character. I believe the present London University Sports Ground club house, Motspur Park, was his home.

The major change in this area of Malden/Old Malden came with the building of the railway line from Raynes Park to Motspur Park, Malden Manor, Tolworth, Chessington North and Chessington South. The railway opened up a hinterland around Malden Manor, very little developed until recent years.

Plough Green itself has been described as an "oasis" in suburbia. It is part of a Kingston borough preservation area and takes the name of the historic Plough Inn, once the haunt of highwaymen, including the dashing Jerry Abershawe, whose "work area" was Putney Heath, Putney Vale, Coombe Woods and on to Malden. A secret room was discovered at the Plough Inn when it was refurbished some years ago. It was in this room, it was thought, that Jerry used to hide from time to time.

The Groves

The birthplace of New Malden is the area of roads known as The Groves on the Coombe Hill side of New Malden railway bridge—a double bridge to accommodate the Kingston line and the Surbiton route. After the opening of Malden's railway station, a group of London businessmen noted the prospects of housing on a "country estate" accessible to town by rail, and The Groves materialised.

A map made in 1867 shows Acacia Grove, Chestnut Grove, Lime Grove, Sycamore Grove, Poplar Walk (now Grove) and Elm Grove (now Elm Road) just as they are today—excepting that 110 years ago there were scarcely any houses in the area. There were, however, a tiny church, a chapel and a gasworks. The rest of New Malden was still a dream, with the exception of a group of cottages and villas at the top end of what is now Cleveland Road and in Providence Place (now Grafton Road).

Legend has it that the Cleveland Road houses were used by the militia: the cottages for the troops and the villas for the officers and their families. Far-fetched though that may seem, it is possible in view of the age of the cottages and villas, and also the fact that the second Earl of Liverpool (1770-1828), who was Prime Minister from 1812-27, lived at Coombe House, Coombe Hill, during his premiership. He died there from a stroke in 1828. His government conducted the Napoleonic Wars to a successful conclusion but the repressive domestic policies which they adopted aroused such opposition that from 1815 to 1820 revolution frequently seemed imminent. Were troops stationed in Cleveland Road to protect the Prime Minister's home, if not his person?

The Groves became the religious, scholastic and artistic centre of embryo New Malden.

The town's first (and only) gasworks was established in 1857 near the junction of Chestnut Grove and Elm Grove. The works were described as "a serious nuisance" and were ultimately purchased by Kingston Gas Company, which connected its mains with the service pipes in New Malden in July 1868. Public lamps were erected and the village roads were lit by gas for the first time.

The little St James's Church, which was superseded by today's Christ Church, was in Poplar Walk. The present Christ Church was consecrated by the Bishop of Winchester in December 1866. The first vicar was the Rev. Charles Stirling, who also became the first chairman of the Maldens and Coombe Urban District Council. Mr Stirling was vicar of Christ Church for twenty-seven years.

The first Christ Church school was opened in March 1867, in the now-replaced St James's Church. For the growing neighbourhood, the building proved inadequate and the Christ Church school for girls and infants was built in Lime Grove in 1870. The old church building was used for boys until the new Lime Grove school was enlarged in 1871. The boys section was again enlarged in 1885, accommodation then being available for 160 boys, 150 girls and 90 infants.

In 1896, to meet growing demands for more room in the infants school, a Church of England boys school was opened in Elm Road by the Bishop of Rochester. The land had been given by the Duke of Cambridge. Today, these Christ Church schools have all been completely modernised and enlarged to meet modern standards.

The original Baptist chapel, built in the garden of a house in Poplar Walk (now Poplar Grove) is the forerunner of today's fine Baptist Church, Kingston Road, rebuilt after complete destruction in the second world war during a daylight bombing attack on Malden.

The earliest records of The Groves artistic and theatrical lustre have come to me through two sisters: Miss Cecil Rough, teacher of music, and Miss Agnes Rough.

The first two houses built in The Groves were Beaulah Villa and its neighbour Perth Villa (now Nos. 48 and 50 Chestnut Grove). They were erected about 1864 by a Mr Penny who was killed by falling from scaffolding on the site during their construction.

Mr George Hogg and his wife (great-uncle and great-aunt of the Misses Rough) came to live in Beaulah Villa about 1866. In a bungalow near the Hoggs lived Mr Augustus Harris, an impressario at Covent Garden Opera House. He used to invite operatic singers down to enjoy the country air in New Malden. Among the illustrious visitors was Madame Adelina Patti, the famous soprano. A present-day link between Acacia Grove and the theatre is Fred Emney, the comedy actor. His father, also a celebrated actor, lived in Acacia Grove and the family home was a rendezvous for stage stars. Malden was chosen by many stage people because of the almost continuous twenty-hour hour train service to London.

Incidentally, I discovered that the comedian Max Wall, recently described as "finest among our living clowns" was a pupil at Christ Church School, Elm Road.

"His real name was Lorimer and he was known as Maxie Lorimer to us," said Mr Wilfred Wiles, chairman of Malden Civic Society, who was a classmate of the comedian during their schooldays. "At the Elm Road school he always had a group of boys around him in the playground listening to his tall stories and to his store of fantasies. I suppose we were lucky to have someone like him in the class to relieve the boredom of school life in those days. It was all very serious indeed—and Max was like a breath of fresh air. The Lorimer family, stage folk, lived in Lime Grove."

In the realm of fine art, a Victorian house now called The Lodge, in Elm Road near the junction with Chestnut Grove, was the home of a noted Victorian animal painter, Mr J. S. Noble. The house, built about 1870, was then called Harwood House.

Malden's Railway Hotel, on the Coombe Road side of the railway station, has a long name-changing history. It was built on the site of the only house in the area when the railway line was laid; this was the home of Mr Harry West, the oldest living inhabitant of that part of the parish, according to contemporary records. In 1852, Mr West's house was converted into the Railway Tavern, kept for many years by Mr Henry Berry and his family. In 1890, the name of the public house was changed to the Railway Hotel, under Mr E. Coxon. In 1895-6, a further change of name gave Station Hotel, under Mr C. Pryor, but by 1897 the name became the Railway Hotel as it is today.

Almost opposite the public house in the days before and possibly during the first world war was the Malden Soup Kitchen. It was housed in a wooden shed which was pulled down when the present Coombe Road entrance to Malden railway station was built. Bones and split peas were used to make the nourishing soup.

I own an elegantly framed presentation picture depicting the interior of an old-fashioned kitchen. Beneath it is the inscription: "With the Compliments of the Committee of New Malden Soup Kitchen 1911-12."

To my own local knowledge, another form of "soup kitchen" existed locally during the last war—the British Restaurants. There was one in Alric House, at the corner of Alric Avenue, and another in St James's Church Hall, Green Lane. These restaurants were not only for those short of money, but for all who wished to eat out at very reasonable prices to assist with food rationing problems.

Incidentally, in Hook Road, Tolworth, there was a splendid soup kitchen around 1900 at The Haven Coffee Rooms and Working-men's Club, today Nos. 170 and 168 Hook Road. The premises were also a local slate club. It was possible to get a night's lodging at The Haven "on the parish" for 2d. including a supper of bread and cheese and cocoa and a good breakfast. The other soup kitchen in the area was at St Paul's Parish Room. At The Haven, a big ewer of hot soup cost 2d.

Coombe Hill

A war hero, a royal duke who defied convention by marrying an actress and a Prime Minister who had a longer single term of office than any other Cabinet leader are among the personalities who make the Malden slopes of Coombe Hill a fascinating area for research.

It was not until the 1930s that building development in the Clarence Avenue, Darley Drive and Buxton Drive area extended urbanisation and transformed the meadows of Coombe House, the former centre of the royal Cambridge estate.

Until the late 1930s, the territory joining today's Elm Road and Clarence Avenue was sports fields owned by Whitbread's Brewery and by Burberry's Ltd., the weatherproof garment manufacturers. At one time a tree-fringed pond was in this area, the water draining into the stream which now goes underground to drain finally into Beverley Brook.

The wooden building which was for some years the Barton Green Youth Centre, and is now used by Blagdon Venture Scout Unit and the Malden Youth Theatre Group, was originally Whitbread's sports pavilion. There were some quite magnificent iron gates across the former end of Elm Road, at the entrance to the Whitbread sports ground.

Today, the Kingston by-pass cuts in two the parish of St James's Church.

Today, the Whitbread and Burberry grounds form the site of the Barton Green housing development and open space dedicated to the memory of one of Malden's Victoria Cross airmen: Flying Officer Cyril Joe Barton, V.C., a former Beverley School pupil. The Barton Library and Resources Centre at Beverley School is also dedicated to his memory. His photograph and an extract from the Victoria Cross citation can be seen by the staircase at Malden Branch Library. Beside it is the photograph and citation of his companion Victoria Cross holder, Squadron Leader Ian Willoughby Bazalgette, after whom Bazalgette Gardens housing development off South Lane, Malden, is named.

Adolphus and George, Dukes of Cambridge

When the Dukes of Cambridge were associated with Coombe Hill, aeroplanes had not yet been invented, and both were army men. The son, George, was Commander-in-Chief of the army for almost forty years. He was much interested in New Malden's development, although I can find no trace that either he or his father actually lived at Coombe. He gave the site of Christ Church, its vicarage and the site of the church schools to local people.

The Coombe House meadows, including the site of the present Coombe Girls School, Clarence Avenue, were used for local jollifications, including Fire Brigade displays and horticultural shows. The meadows were also used by shooting parties which included such illustrious guests as King Edward VII. A local Ordnance Survey map dated as late as 1913 shows a "pheasantry" as a row of little huts just off what is now Neville Avenue, Coombe Hill.

King Edward VII frequently stayed at various society houses in the area. He was fond of shooting—and sometimes his language was as robust as his figure. The late Mr Frank Herbert of Grafton Road, Malden, used to act as a beater with other lads "from the village" during the King's pheasant shoots. "We were bobbing up and down in the corn one day trying to get a better look when the King came over and shouted, 'Get your bloody heads down or you will get them shot off!' "

The actress Lily Langtry, much admired by King Edward VII, lived for a time on Kingston Hill in a house overlooking Richmond Park.

Another actress, Miss Louisa Fairbrother, became the morganatic wife of Prince George, Duke of Cambridge, and will always be remembered in Malden by Fitzgeorge Avenue. The former Fitzgeorge School, Kingston Road, was also named after her. The Duke married Louisa in the face of tremendous opposition, having sworn as a young man that he would "only marry for love." Louisa took no part in her husband's official life. He kept the two worlds separate but their letters testify to their undying love. They were ideally happy and celebrated their golden wedding anniversary before her death in 1890.

They had three sons, Colonel George FitzGeorge, Rear-Admiral Sir Adolphus FitzGeorge and Colonel Augustus FitzGeorge. The present Coombe Wood golf course, off George Road, Coombe, was constructed for them by the Duke of Cambridge. The course, now owned by Kingston Council and leased to the present club, was opened to members in 1904. The Prime Minister, Mr Arthur Balfour, drove the first "public ball" and became the club's first captain. He was followed as captain by the Duke of Cambridge's second son in 1905 and by his third son in 1921.

Mrs FitzGeorge's homes were at No. 6 Queen Street, Mayfair, and in the country at Cambridge Lodge, Horley. It is doubtful if she ever lived in Coombe. An exceptionally beautiful woman, she was noted for her charming personality and gentle ways.

Considerable researches into the Coombe Manor estate, how it was bought by the old Duke of Cambridge from Earl Spencer, original owner of today's Wimbledon Common area, have been made over the past five or so years by Mr Lionel Gent of Kenley Road, Kingston, member of Kingston Archaeological Society. His investigations included searches in Spencer archives.

Coombe House, incidentally, was pulled down to make room for housing development well after the end of the last war. The house overlooked the whole of the New Malden area. Its carriage drives now form Fitzgeorge Avenue and part of Warren Rise at the top of Coombe Hill. It was the home for many years, until his death in 1828, of the second Earl of Liverpool, Prime Minister for fifteen consecutive years (1812-27).

During the Earl of Liverpool's residence at Coombe House, he entertained there the Prince Regent, the King of Prussia and leading generals of the day including Field Marshal Blucher, who defeated Napoleon at Ligny and shared with Wellington the triumph at Waterloo.

To Mr Sydney Ripley, Kingston's representative in the G.L.C., I am indebted for this anecdote of Blucher. On returning to London from visiting Coombe House, the Field Marshal was taken to an eminence from which he could look down on London. His comment was: "What a wonderful city to sack!"

Personalities of Coombe Hill

The story of Coombe Hill begins with the Romans and continues through centuries of rural peace before its discovery as a prestige building site in the mid-1800s.

A number of Roman articles have been found over the years in the area of the present Coombe Wood golf course. When the Romans forded the Thames at Kingston, they camped on high ground: the present Coombe area.

Centuries passed, and this crest of Coombe Hill remained the territory of birds and wild animals. One of the first to see the possibilities of building on this near-to-London rural site was John Galsworthy, father of the author of *The Forsyte Saga* and other notable books.

It is after this author that the road by Kingston Hospital, previously part of Gloucester Road, was renamed Galsworthy Road in commemoration of the centenary of his birth. He lived from 1867-1933. He was, incidentally, born at Parkfield, a Victorian mansion still standing on Kingston Hill. John Galsworthy senior was a London solicitor who had married a young woman from Surbiton, Miss Blanche Bailey Bartlett, in 1862. After the birth of the first child, Lilian, they moved from their Portland Place home in London to Parkfield. This house is just beyond today's Ladderstile pedestrian crossing on the road from Kingston to Kingston Vale.

While at Parkfield, John Galsworthy senior purchased twenty-four acres of Coombe Hill fronting George Road. His career as a house builder makes me feel a pang of pity for his wife and family. In turn, John Galsworthy senior built three fine mansions along the road, and the family moved from one to the other and then back again to the second-built house; and all in the space of a few years, too, for the family moved away from Coombe in 1886.

Two of the houses Galsworthy senior built are still there. These are his second house, then Coombe Leigh, now Coombe Ridge House, and the Holy Cross Convent Preparatory School, George Road (it was for some years the Holy Family Preparatory School). The other house is Coombe Croft, now Rokeby School, the boys preparatory school which moved to Coombe in 1966 when the previous premises in Wimbledon were purchased by Merton Council.

The "missing" house of the Galsworthy trio is the first-built house, Coombe Warren. It was the central house of the three and had a distinguished record of society entertaining. After the Galsworthys sold it, the house belonged for a number of years to Lord Ripon, who enlarged the premises and called the house Coombe Court. It was the scene of lavish parties and brilliant entertainments, including visits from Edward VII and Queen Alexandra. The house was pulled down in 1931 to make room for building development.

Several houses now in the area bear names reminiscent of *The Forsyte Saga*. Although John Galsworthy, the author, moved from Coombe with his family soon after he left Harrow School, he never forgot his childhood home. He set the Forsyte stories in the Coombe of his memories.

In a letter written in 1929, Galsworthy stated: "The site of the Forsyte house was the site of my father's Coombe Warren, the grounds and the coppice, etc., were actual but the house itself I built with my imagination . . . " The pond by which the Forsyte characters Irene Soames and architect Bossiney "made the plunge of acknowledging their love" can still be seen. It is the lower end of The Drive, a turning off George Road through territory which was once the grounds of Coombe Warren. Today, although almost ringed by modern houses, the lake is still beautiful.

The house that the Galsworthy family moved back to, Coombe Ridge, was also the scene of much entertaining. It was the home for a number of years of Sir Frederick Pascoe Rutter, a leading figure in British and international insurance. In 1928, it was the scene of a splendid garden party for the Chartered Insurance Institute Conference.

Another leading businessman who found Coombe Hill an attractive home was Sir Richard Tangye, an ancestor of the contemporary author, Derek Tangye. Sir Richard lived in a house called Gilbertstone.

He was a "captain of industry" and a self-made man whose autobiography is a narrative of struggle and triumph. The book is called *One and All,* a title which is the county motto of Cornwall.

Tangye's Cornwall Works, Smethwick, made engineering history. He had been inspired to become an engineer after seeing as a child one of Britain's first railway engines in service on a line which ran past his father's farm in Cornwall. It was the Tangye hydraulic jacks which enabled Cleopatra's Needle, the obelisk now on the Thames embankment, to be brought to London from Egypt in 1877.

Another interesting house on Coombe Hill is the former home of the Charter Mayor of Malden and Coombe, the late Major John Hill. It adjoins Coombe Hill Golf Course and came to Malden—piece by piece—from Colchester.

In 1962, when the house, known as Coombe Woodhouse, was threatened with demolition, local outcry resulted in its being saved. Inquiries were made as to whether Surrey County Council would purchase the building, but their advisor on historic and antique buildings stated that only about a quarter of the building had actually come from Colchester. The rest was of new materials added when the house was re-erected in Coombe.

Its story, however, is fascinating. The house was originally built in 1483 on the banks of the Colne, near Colchester. It was reputed to have been occupied at one time by Catherine Parr, King Henry VIII's last wife. In 1912, the house was carefully taken to pieces and re-erected in Coombe. The man responsible for the quite literal "house removal" was Mr Walter Thornton Smith, reputed to have made a fortune on the stock exchange. He paid £30,000 for the removal of the house from Colchester and its re-erection.

The architect in charge was Mr J. A. Sherman, who used a splendid system of numbering beams and materials so that they were replaced in the same position.

After the Tudor days of splendour, the fortunes of the house had declined. By the time it was bought by Mr Thornton Smith, it had become a public house called Perseverance. It had been owned by the Colchester Brewery Company and later by Ind Coope Ltd. Essex County Record Office holds plans of its fifteenth and sixteenth century design. It was on these that Mr Sherman based his fine model which Mr Thornton Smith approved before removal—by road—of the ancient house began.

When the present house was threatened in 1962 by demolition for property development, Mr Thornton Smith was living at Shoppenhangers Manor, Maidenhead, later an hotel. He had retired in 1954 from being managing director of Fortnum and Mason's store, Piccadilly. He wrote a vehement letter of criticism to the Malden and Coombe Borough Council who had declared the house "of no historic significance." After stating its history, he ended, "Your misrepresentation is such that one wonders if there can be any ulterior motive?"

In 1924, the house was bought by Sir Ernest Horlick. Later it became the property of Major Hill. It was sold again in 1954. Before demolition was threatened much of the grounds had been sold for property development.

Coombe Wood and Coombe Hill Golf Courses

The nearby Coombe Hill Golf Course, now owned by Kingston Council and leased to the club, was opened in 1911. It had been the property of the Coombe-FitzGeorge estate, the trust administering the territories which had belonged to Prince George, Duke of Cambridge.

Without warning, there appeared in 1931 a printed notice in various parts of Coombe which indicated that Colonel Sir Augustus FitzGeorge, third son of the late duke, then aged over eighty, and his trustees were about to sell both Coombe Wood Golf Course (off George Road) and Coombe Hill Golf Course for building purposes.

Over the years, Sir Augustus had spent much time in residence at Cambridge House, adjoining the Coombe Wood course, which had been laid out originally for his two brothers and himself.

It was proposed that a hundred houses should be erected on the Coombe Wood course and a much larger number on the Coombe Hill course.

After negotiations lasting a year or more, the Coombe-FitzGeorge Trust sold the two golf courses along with some five hundred acres of land towards Kingston Vale and beyond to a London firm of building contractors. After another year's negotiations, Maldens and Coombe Urban District Council were able to assist in a scheme whereby the two golf courses were purchased for £78,000 (including expenses incurred while preparing the case for the Act of Parliament to preserve the use of the ground as open spaces in perpetuity).

Both courses came under the ownership of the Royal Borough of Kingston upon Thames with the creation of the Greater London Council in 1965.

Warren Road

The preservation of the amenities of Coombe Hill is the special responsibility, on behalf of the property owners, of the Malden and Coombe Residents Association Ltd., a non-profit-making company limited by guarantee and not having a share capital. It is this company which issues the car-sticker residents' passes to the area and appoints the gateman at the junction of Warren Road and Coombe Lane West. He is empowered to stop unauthorised traffic from using the private roads of Coombe Hill.

At the Kingston Hill end of Warren Road, almost opposite Fairlawn, Coombe Oaks and the Amy Woodgate Borough Council homes for old people, is the imposing Edwardian mansion, Warren House, now owned by I.C.I. This was the home of General Sir Arthur Henry Fitzroy Paget, who died in December 1928. Until 1956, it was also the home of the late Lady Muriel Paget, famed for her philanthropic work, particularly in Russia and in Yugoslavia where her husband was British Ambassador for a period. Under her direction, Warren House became a convalescent hospital during the last war and afterwards a haven for refugees, housing at one time all the principal members of the ex-government of Yugoslavia, then in exile.

Also on the Kingston-Vale–Beverley-Brook side of Warren Road was the world-famous Veitches Nursery, to which plant collectors sent many rare specimens. It was called Coombe Wood Nursery and today many of the fine houses in that area of Coombe owe the magnificent trees in their gardens to specimens planted when the nursery flourished. The geographical name of the area is Coombe Ridge.

From time immemorial there had been a public footpath right-of-way on today's Warren Road. In 1853, however, the Duke of Cambridge was advised he had the right to exclude walkers as well as carriage folk. The dispute was settled at Croydon Sessions—and the Duke lost.

The event was celebrated with much jubilation in Kingston. At the time New Malden and Coombe were part of the old Royal Borough of Kingston. It was Kingston Council's Alderman Frederick Gould who led the fight to keep Coombe open.

It was not until December 1866 that Malden's Local Board was set up following the passing of an Act of Parliament of 1855 which defined the limits of Kingston's borough boundary. By a strange oversight this Act resulted in New Malden receiving payments for rates on the Surrey portion of Kingston bridge and from Hook residents as well as from Coombe. The position was rectified at a meeting held at Kingston's Town Hall (now the Market Hall) in February 1867.

The Coombe Estate

The present day Coombe Manor is a case of mixed identity. Today, the New Victoria Hospital, Coombe Lane West, has fine wrought-iron gates embellished with the name Coombe Manor. It was the name given to the mansion, a fairly new property, by its former owner. But the original Coombe Manor house was centuries old. It was on the site of the Coombe House of which only the substantial garden walls fronting Traps Lane remain. The lower part of these walls are of Tudor brick.

Legend has it that this road was named after a Madam Trap. She is shown by the Poor Rate Books in the 1758 era as renting a house and garden in the vicinity. Old maps show the road, however, as being Coombe Road right down the hill to what is now Malden Fountain roundabout.

Today's Coombe Road is a small stretch of road joining Traps Lane to Malden High Street, and is between Christ Church and the British Rail station—now called New Malden Station.

To return to the first Coombe Manor. As it was the only house in the area, it had no actual name, I learn from Mr Lionel Gent of Kingston Archaeological Society. The lands were the Manor of Coombe, and the house had been owned by the Lord of the Manor for hundreds of years. Earl Spencer, Lord of the Manor in the early 1800s, sold it with the Manor lands to Prince Adolphus, Duke of Cambridge. The Coombe-FitzGeorge estate, as the Manor became, was not broken up until the building boom of the 1930s, as described earlier.

Incidentally, the Domesday Book gives the area as belonging to "Humphrey the Chamberlain". The name Coombe is said to derive from the Welsh word "Cwm," meaning a wooded valley, which seems to imply that Coombe at one time covered a much larger area. In 1320, the daughters of William de Nevill bestowed the lands on their husbands and the area became known as Coombe Nevill, as today's Neville Avenue, off Traps Lane, recalls.

The old Manor of Coombe lands passed eventually to Merton Priory, probably by bequests. When Henry VIII confiscated monastic property, Coombe become Crown land.

Queen Elizabeth I gave the manorial rights to Sir William Cecil in 1562. He passed them on to his friend Sir Thomas Vincent. In 1602, the year before she died, Queen Elizabeth I visited the Manor of Coombe. The old house was pulled down in 1753 by Earl Spencer, and Coombe House, later the home of the Earl of Liverpool, the famous prime minister, was built.

In 1887 Coombe House was enjoying considerable fame as a "health farm" under a Dr McGeagh, J.P. It was described as a "charming establishment" by Mr F. Somner Merryweather, chairman for many years of Maldens and Coombe Urban District Council.

Nijinsky, most famous of all Diaghilev's Russian dancers, was a guest at Lady Gladys Ripon's home Coombe Court (formerly the Galsworthy home Coombe Warren), George Road. Lady Ripon was a devotee of ballet and she and her daughter, Lady Juliet Duff, travelled to Paris and to New York for Nijinsky's performances.

Queen Alexandra was also a frequent visitor to Coombe Court. She was a close friend of Lady Ripon, daughter of the Sidney Herbert who helped Florence Nightingale to establish her military hospital in Scutari during the Crimean War.

Towards the end of her life, Lady Ripon became fatally ill with cancer. Many of her friends no longer came to Coombe, but Queen Alexandra was faithful to the last. After spending some time on each visit with Lady Ripon, she would walk alone in tears round the small lake which is now in the grounds of a house in The Drive, a short road

Fig. 15   Mrs. Ford's stall, once opposite the Bonesgate public house.

Fig. 16 Oil Mill Lane, now Villiers Road, Kingston.

Fig. 17 Malden's unlucky fountain—it was knocked down twice.

Fig. 18 Christ Church, New Malden, as planned.

which goes across the site of Coombe Court and its gardens.

Melba, the Australian Queen of Song, was for a time a resident on Coombe Hill. She rented Coombe Cottage, now 187 Coombe Lane West, the premises (much enlarged) of Rediffusion Engineering Ltd.

It was in fact Lady Ripon (when Lady de Grey, before her husband succeeded to the title of the Marquess of Ripon) who first brought Melba to the Covent Garden Opera House. She had heard Melba sing in Brussels in 1887. Lady de Grey was a member of the committee which encouraged the staging of grand opera at Covent Garden by ensuring that the costs of each season were covered by advance subscriptions.

When Melba finally returned to Australia to create a home base for her opera tours, she named that home Coombe Cottage, to recall her Coombe Hill days. The "Aussie" Coombe Cottage was at Coldstream, not far from Melbourne.

Melba had rented the English Coombe Cottage for "one lovely summer" from Admiral Lord Charles Beresford, a close friend of King Edward VII. Another distinguished occupant of the house was Mr Baring, subsequently Lord Revelstoke.

Adjoining the present Rediffusion premises are Coombe Hill Riding School Stables, a picturesque reminder of earlier days. Whether they were the stables belonging to Coombe Cottage (a misnomer for a house of twenty bedrooms) or for the almost adjoining Coombe Warren mansion is hard to say.

The lodge to Coombe Warren is now an impressive residence itself, by modern standards. It is at the junction of Coombe Hill Road and Coombe Lane West. The Lodge was known colloquially for many years as "the postcard house" as it featured on the local views so beloved by our grandparents.

For a time Coombe Warren was the home of Mr and Mrs Bertram Woodhouse-Currie. When her husband died in 1896 at the age of sixty-nine, Mrs Caroline Louisa Currie built St Agatha's Roman Catholic Church, Kings Road, Kingston, in his memory. Tablets to both man and wife are in the church, which is a splendid example of late Victorian architecture. It was built alongside Kingston Barracks to serve the needs of local Catholics, many of whom had returned as wives to the soldiers when the regiment came back to Kingston after service in Ireland.

King Edward VII was a frequent visitor to another house in the area: Coombe Springs, the home of Mrs Hufwa Williams, whose husband was a founder of Sandown Racecourse. Coombe Springs, now demolished, is the site of Lord Chancellor Walk, off Coombe Lane West.

Mrs Williams was a woman of character and enterprise, who liked all her guests to be active, and is once said to have bullied

Edward VII into painting a garden seat on one of his visits.

Coombe Springs narrowly escaped becoming the setting for a siege. A frequent guest at Mrs Williams' house was Prince Felix Youssoupoff, one of the men who plotted the death of Rasputin. At one time the Prince was taking a collection of English cattle home to Russia to improve the stock on the family farm. They were allowed to graze at Coombe Springs before journeying to Russia. Mrs Hufwa Williams grew attached to the animals and threatened to put her home into a stage of siege to protect the cattle, However, she was eventually persuaded that Russia had the greater claim.

Although Coombe Springs House is no more, its famous Conduit House, central point of Cardinal Wolsey's Hampton Court water system, remains. It is now in a private garden. The last owners before building development took place were the Sufi Community, purchasers of the estate from the Institute of Comparative Study of History, Philosophy and the Sciences, directed by the late Mr John Godolphin Bennett, a most remarkable man. He took over the property from Mrs Hufwa Williams in 1941 for use as laboratories for the British Coal Utilisation Research Association. The great scientist, Lord Rutherford, chairman of the Government's Advisory Council for Scientific and Industrial Research, was closely involved in the project.

At the same time, Mr Bennett conducted research on a spiritual level into the "system," the name given to the teaching and methods learned by Mr Bennett and his companions from Gurdjieff as transmitted by Ouspensky.

After a number of years, the Government transferred the coal laboratories to Leatherhead, but the Institute set up by Mr Bennett continued until it moved first to Brunswick Road, Kingston, and later into the country.

One of the most remarkable features of the Institute's stay in Coombe Springs was the building of a hall, praised in design by the eminent American architect, Frank Lloyd Wright. This building, called Djamichunnatra, was for the performance of spiritual exercises. It was built by the community living at Coombe Springs and was pulled down to make way for the houses now in Lord Chancellor Walk. Adherents of Subud came to Coombe Springs in 1957. Seminars at the house and in its subsidiary buildings were held regularly and hundreds attended the international conferences, usually held annually.

New Malden Farms

Railways and tramways created a new Kingston, linked with the outside world and ready for the twentieth century.

Before the coming of the railways, Kingston, Surbiton and Malden were sleepy rural communities. By the mid-1800s this pleasant life had begun to change. The metamorphosis started in 1838 for Surbiton, 1846 for Malden and 1863 for Kingston—the years when they received railway stations. But the farms remained prosperous for some years, until property developers offered attractive prices when building houses to tempt Londoners to a "country residence."

In New Malden, for example, there were a number of farms actively engaged in mixed agriculture. For instance, Hoppingwood Farm (the original farm is now vanished and is replaced by Cambridge Avenue, Hoppingwood Avenue, Rosebery Avenue and surrounding roads in New Malden); Coombe Wood Farm (now called Hoppingwood Farm), by the junction of Coombe Lane West and the Kingston by-pass; Blue House Farm (in the area of Beverley School, Blake's Lane and Blake's Avenue); and New House Farm, at the corner of South Lane, then called Sow Lane.

I have a lovely water-colour painting of New House Farm and tree-lined South Lane painted in 1924 by H. Alexander. It was on view at the Malden Rotary Club exhibition "Malden When New" at Malden Adult Education Centre.

The original Hopping Wood recalled by the names of these farms was once part of Coombe Wood, bisected by the Kingston by-pass. Local folk-lore suggests that the Hopping Wood was named after the many song birds that frequented the area. Beverley Brook is said to be named after beavers which once populated its banks.

Blakes Farm presents a real mystery. Was it once the site of a Roman villa? Several older residents maintain they played fivestones as children with pieces of Roman tessellated pavement. This seems quite likely, bearing in mind the fact that many Roman remains have been found on Coombe Hill and in the vicinity of the playing fields of Malden Parochial School. Mr H. Carpenter, headmaster of that school for many years, was an enthusiastic archaeologist and mapped Roman finds over a considerable area in the Manor Drive vicinity.

One of the most notable buildings on the former Blakes Farm land, in what is now Welbeck Close, was Malden College. This distinguished building had a singular history. It was a boarding and day school prior to the first world war, then it was for a time a wartime clothing factory. After the war it was called St George's College (1928-32). It was finally reopened under the original name of Malden College in one of the big houses which have now been replaced by St James's Close.

Richmond Park

Richmond Park, like Warren Road, narrowly escaped being closed to the public. Although a peaceful area now, the Ladderstile

Gate and the name Ladderstile Ride, Kingston Hill, recall a bitterly fought contest.

When Richmond Park was originally enclosed by King Charles I for hunting purposes, six gates were made. The name Coombe Gate was given to the original gate at today's Ladderstile entrance.

In 1747, Princess Amelia, the youngest daughter of King George II, was appointed Ranger of Richmond Park. She took up residence in White Lodge, and, very shortly after taking up her appointment, closed the park to the public and refused admission except to her personal friends and those few others with special permits which were difficult to obtain.

Ladderstile Gate (or Coombe Gate) featured in an action for right-of-way brought in 1754. The two-day case was heard by the Lord Chief Justice and a jury. It was lost by the plaintiffs after thirty-seven witnesses testified that anyone willing to pay 2s. 6d. (a good sum in those days) could buy a key to the park.

In the following year, a Richmond brewer, Mr John Lewis, tried to enter the park as an ordinary pedestrian. He was ejected and subsequently brought an action challenging Princess Amelia's right of exclusion. After three years of procrastination, the case was heard at Kingston Surrey Assizes on 3 April 1758. Lewis based his case on the rights-of-way granted to pedestrians by King Charles I—and he won it. Asked by the judge whether he would have admission by gates or stepladders, he said he preferred ladders since gate keys could be lost.

Forced to put up ladderstiles, the Princess angrily insisted that very widely spaced rungs were used, making the ladder extremely difficult to climb.

Brewer Lewis again applied to the court and the judge ordered that the rungs of the ladders were to be no farther apart than could be used by old people and children. A third action, in 1760, to secure the rights of admission to Richmond Park for carriages without tickets went in favour of the Crown.

So far as our Ladderstile Gate is concerned, it was the last real ladder "gate" to the park. It was not made into a foot-gate until 1884-5. The present cradle gate for pedestrians was substituted for the foot gate in 1901.

Malden's Wartime Role

Coombe Hill and its imposing residences—including General Eisenhower's hideaway at Telegraph Cottage, Warren Road—were next door to the device which made Malden a "decoy town" to the Germans in the second world war. These decoys were, at the time, a military secret. They were devices which automatically opened and produced a flame when enemy aricraft came within a range of six miles. They frequently misled enemy pilots into thinking they represented factory sites which had been set alight by early bombers, thus diverting aeroplanes from authentic targets.

The Kingston–Malden site of the decoy was in Richmond Park, near the Penn Ponds, within easy walking distance of Coombe Hill. Malden's tragic record of heavy bombardment may, in part, have been due to the presence of the decoy diverting bombers from London itself.

For many years, the repeated bombing of local sites was attributed to the fact that South London's main water supply passes through the town just by the railway line, *en route* from Surbiton water works to London. The bombardments started with the devastating daylight raid of 16 August 1940—the first daylight raid by German bombers on London during the last war. In the raid, heavy casualties were sustained, and over 1,300 houses were damaged, 84 being either totally destroyed or so badly damaged that they had to be demolished. Between this raid and the end of the war, practically every property in the area received damage in some degree from bomb attack.

A booklet called *Trial by Ordeal: Malden Faces Total War* was published some years ago by the former Malden and Coombe Borough Council.

Telegraph Cottage, the home of Mrs Gabrielle Keiller, Warren Road, is much altered since it was used by General Eisenhower as a country retreat from the London headquarters, during the planning of D-Day, when Supreme Commander of the Allied Forces in Europe. The house has been much enlarged since Eisenhower's day, although the underground dug-out where D-Day plans were discussed still remains. It was at nearby Castlecombe, an elegant mansion, that Churchill stayed from time to time during conferences with Eisenhower.

In 1976, Malden and Coombe Civic Society was instrumental in having a plaque placed on Telegraph Cottage to permanently record General Eisenhower's stay. It was unveiled by the Mayor, Councillor Frank Steptoe, in the presence of Mrs Keiller and Mr Wilfred Wiles, chairman of the Civic Society, and many spectators present at an open day in aid of the Retired District Nurses Fund and of the National Trust Gardens.

Although named Telegraph Cottage, it is unlikely that it was ever used as a message-sending point on the relay chain from the Admiralty to Portsmouth. An earlier semaphore station was situated on what appears to have been later the Coombe Wood Golf Course, according to early maps. The semaphore station closed following the invention of the Morse Code by the American Samuel F. B. Morse (1791-1872).

Kingston Hill

Kingston Hill, cradle of the borough, was the site of a church-and-people festival in 1976 to celebrate the centenary of St Paul's Church.

It was Kingston Hill that the first settlers chose when they came to the area. This high ground overlooking the Thames attracted early man before ever that river was named. When the Romans came nearly 2,000 years ago they forded the river more or less where Kingston Bridge is today. In early times, the river was wider and shallower. Roman implements found on Kingston Hill can be seen in the town's museum, Fairfield West. As life became more secure in Saxon times, the township of Cyningestun in the region of Suthregia (as Kingston was then called) was the site of a great council held in 838 by King Egbert. At this time, Kingston Hill was a stretch of open common-land, crossed by a cart-track to London on the route of today's Kingston Hill road.

The story of the building of St. Paul's Church is the saga of the rehabilitation of the Kingston Hill area.

The original church, made of corrugated iron, was built in 1870. It was a daughter church of St. Peter's Church, Norbiton. The church was at the corner of Park Road and Elm Road, Kingston. The man who founded the new little church was the Rev. A. Cornford, then a curate at St Peter's. He had special responsibility for the area which is now St Paul's and St. Luke's parishes. He had been at St Peter's for four years when he became convinced of the need to provide a new place for church worship. He therefore paid for the iron church out of his own pocket—£500 or £600 (a big sum in those days).

At the same time, the Rev Cornford also had the first St Paul's day school built, again at his own expense. Soon the school became too small and a new school was built at a cost of £2,000.

Before long, it became clear that the iron church was inadequate for the needs of the district but, before a fund could be launched to build something bigger, a debt of £600 on the rebuilt church school had to be cleared. Here, again, the Rev. Cornford stepped into the breach, and paid the debt himself. He was repaid ten years later.

The foundation stone of today's St Paul's Church was laid on 10 June 1876, by Princess Mary Adelaide, Duchess of Teck (and mother of Queen Mary). She was living at White Lodge, Richmond Park, at that time.

The site of the church cost £500. As there was only £2,700 in hand, it was decided that only the nave and the aisles should be built. They were to cost £4,500 and would accommodate 664 people as against 833 in the full plan. The population of the district at that time was about 5,000.

On October 18 1877, the present St Paul's Church was opened by the Bishop of Guildford. Because there was a debt of about £1,500 on the building, the church was licensed but not consecrated.

The font was provided by money collected by the children of the parish. The lectern—a splendid brass eagle—was given by Mr John Galsworthy (senior), father of John Galsworthy, the author. At the time the family were living in George Road, Kingston Hill. Because the eagle, although splendid, was inclined to be a rather top-heavy perch for the Bible, the present handrails, steps and dais were given to the church in 1939 by the late Mr Leonard H. Bentall, father of Bentall's present chairman.

St Paul's was consecrated on 30 October 1880 and the Rev. Cornford was instituted as the first vicar. In 1908, the vicarage was purchased, adjoining the church, and a scheme was set afoot for the completion of the church.

In 1924, a new church bell was obtained. It was formerly the ship's bell of *H.M.S. Conqueror.* In 1928, the church received its first curate, the Rev. Roy McKay, later to become Director of Religious Programmes for the B.B.C.

The ministry of Canon Arthur Wellesley Orr at St. Paul's far exceeded in length that of any other clergyman at the church. He was appointed in 1923. His successor, the Rev. R. L. Wild, did not take over until forty years later, in 1963. The vicars after the Rev. A. Cornford were the Rev. J. Lemon (appointed 1887), the Rev. E. S. Shuttleworth (1903) and then the Rev. Wellesley Orr twenty years later. The present vicar, the Rev. George Cutcher, came to St. Paul's in 1974.

Beside ancient history, Kingston Hill has a Tudor claim to fame. A site at today's junction between Crescent Road and Kingston Hill was the place where a Roman Catholic priest met a violent death in the reign of Queen Elizabeth I.

A determined effort to have the priest canonised as a saint is being made by a number of Roman Catholics led by Father John Cremin of St Agatha's Church, Kings Road. Kingston Hill is in the parish of this church and of its daughter church, St Anne's, near the Gipsy Hill Department of Kingston Polytechnic.

The priest was William Way. He was put to death in a cruel and vicious way on 23 September 1588. A pamphlet describing the event and preceding circumstances has been printed and issued by Father Cremin.

"William Way was one of the 160 English martyrs beatified in 1929. He was not among the 40 English and Welsh martyrs selected from this list who were canonised by our present Holy Father, Pope Paul VII, on 25 October 1970."

After recounting how William Way, born in Exeter, was trained for the Roman Catholic priesthood at the English College in Rheims, Father Cremin describes his arrest and imprisonment after a six-month ministry in England. Way was arrested in Lambeth and imprisoned in 1587 in the notorious Clink Prison, Southwark (origin of the slang expression for prison).

He was tried at the Old Bailey on 16 September of that year and, on refusing to abandon his faith, was sentenced to death for being a Roman Catholic priest. The judge who passed sentence was William Fleetwood, at the time Recorder of Kingston.

After being conveyed to Kingston from London by river, Way was taken to gallows erected on Kingston Hill, where he was "hanged and quartered with severity."

It is possible that William Way's gallows were specially constructed and were only used at his demise. Can you picture the scene? The priest, unceasingly proclaiming his faith, was dragged from the Thames-side through the sixteenth century Kingston streets and up the slope of Kingston Hill—at that time looking very much like a "green hill without a city wall".

At a less exalted level, Kingston Hill was for many years the home of the London Zoological Society's country "rest-home" for animals which were off-colour. This country zoo was in the vicinity of what is now Liverpool Road. It backed on to Richmond Park.

In the mid-1850s Kingston townsfolk used to take children to see the animals as a Sunday treat.

Liverpool Road itself is named after the Earl of Liverpool, Prime Minister for fifteen years, who lived at Coombe House. He died in 1828, having relinquished the office of Prime Minister when he suffered a paralytic stroke in 1827.

The Earl's wife died on 12 June 1821. There is a beautiful white marble statue to her memory in All Saints Church, Kingston. Coombe in those days was in Kingston parish, as was the area that later became New Malden. The Countess's memorial statute is by the famous Sir Francis Legatt Chantrey (1781-1841). Son of a carpenter, he was apprenticed to a Sheffield carver and gilder.

King Edward VII was a frequent visitor to Kingston Hill, for the beautiful actress Lily Langtry, much admired by the King, lived for a time in Kingston Hill Place, a mansion which became part of Gipsy Hill College of Education and is now part of the Gipsy Hill section of Kingston Polytechnic. The Jersey Lily, as the populace called Mrs Langtry because she had been born in the Channel Islands, was well suited by the elegant house and its fine grounds.

It was for her, I understand, that the massive wall surrounding Richmond Park was breached so that an uninterrupted view of rolling turf, the trees and deer, could be obtained. A ha-ha still forms a ditch separating Kingston Hill Place lawns from Richmond Park. A wire fence, however, now reinforces security. An agreed fee was paid each year to the Richmond Park authorities for this "right to view."

Going from Kingston Hill Place with its royal associations towards Robin Hood Gate, the name of the road changes from Kingston Hill to Kingston Vale. The postal address also changes from Kingston upon Thames to Putney S.W.15.

Despite the preponderance of high society and wealth in the Kingston-Hill–Coombe-Hill area of the Edwardian age, there was a deep sense of responsibility towards others. A Working Men's Institute, with the Duke of Cambridge as president, flourished in Kingston Vale, and, in Malden itself, there were in fact "too many institutions for the size of the place and each languishes for want of support," reported the redoubtable Mr F. Somner Merryweather in his *Half a Century of Kingston History.* "It has its Building Society, its Odd Fellows and other charitable and self-helping Clubs: its Cricket Clubs, its Harriers, its Village Band and its Temperance Societies. A Coffee Tavern and Working Men's Club was opened with much ceremony on 15 September 1880, by H.R.H. Princess Mary, Duchess of Teck, but working men did not support it and the Palm Tree Coffee Tavern is now maintained by the friends of the temperance cause."

The Duchess of Teck lived in White Lodge, Richmond Park. Her daughter was Princess May. There had been local rejoicings for her engagement to Prince Albert, Prince of Wales, who died suddenly before the marriage could take place. She became the wife of his brother, Prince George, later George V. The Duchess was an impressive personality both in character and in size. She and her family worshipped at St. John the Baptist Church, Kingston Vale—and the pew she used was specially widened to accommodate her physique.

A far slimmer royal resident, at least at the time of his stay, was Prince Farouk of Egypt, later King Farouk. As a young lad Prince Farouk lived at Kenry House, now Gipsy Hill College. He stayed there to receive the benefits of an English education under private tutors, having been refused entry to Eton because he knew no Latin.

At the age of sixteen, he received news at Kenry House that his father, King Fuad, had died. He returned at once to Egypt to begin the reign that lasted until he was toppled from his throne by a military coup in 1952. He died from a heart attack in a Rome nightclub in 1965.

Although he returned to Egypt in haste on succeeding to the throne, Farouk returned to Kenry House the following year, 1937, as king, for a sight-seeing tour with his mother, Queen Nazil, and his four younger sisters. He had grown fond of the house during his earlier stay when he was being prepared for entry into the Royal Military Academy, Woolwich.

In those youthful years, he was a slight graceful youth, a shadow of the corpulent monarch of so few years later. Enchanted by English ways, he sent presents home to Egypt by virtually every post during his first stay in Kingston. He dodged his tutors and borrowed a bicycle to go shopping by himself at Bentalls and other stores. There, he would buy little trinkets, including the butterfly wing jewellery, for his sisters. To the local people, he was known as Prince Freddy.

Kenry House still looks just as it did when King Farouk lived there. In fact, it still looks as it did when it was the home of the Earl of Dunraven and Mountearl (1812-71), who became the first Baron Kenry. He was an eminent archaeologist, astronomer and psychic researcher.

Earlier Kenry House had been called Coombe Wood. Because the house is on an eminence, the view from its rooms and gardens is magnificent. The trees of Coombe Wood mask the Kingston by-pass and prevent any houses being seen. It is as if Kenry House were still in the depths of the country. Before being purchased by Surrey County Council, the house was owned by Mr F. S. Oliver.

Today, Kenry House, Coombe Hurst (higher up the hill) and Kingston Hill Place form the Gipsy Hill complex, part of Kingston Polytechnic.

Kingston Vale

Kingston Vale was once known as "Jerry's Hill" after the infamous Coombe Wood highwayman, Louis Jeremiah Abershawe, hanged in 1795 for his misdeeds. One of his hideouts was said to have been a secret room at The Plough, Old Malden. Another was at the original Three Compasses, Eden Street (then Heathen Street), Kingston.

His favourite hunting area was the coaching route down Roehampton Vale, up Kingston Vale, and on to Kingston Hill. There were rich pickings in the eighteenth century on this stretch of the Portsmouth Road.

There was a notorious inn called The Bald-Faced Stag near the present Robin Hood Gate to Richmond Park. It was a rendezvous for certain "gentlemen of the road" who besides Abershawe included William Brown and Joseph Witlock, both hanged at Tyburn in 1773.

Jerry was a "good-looking young man," according to contemporary records. He was eventually captured in a Southwark inn in 1795, after a violent struggle with the Bow Street Runners, and convicted at Croydon Assizes of murdering David Price, one of the officials who had attempted to arrest him. He was hanged on Kennington Common on 3 August 1795, meeting his death bravely, "with his shirt thrown open and a flower in his mouth."

An account states: "On the Sunday following his execution London was like a deserted city; hundreds of thousands went to see him hanging in chains. Later he was long on view, similarly festooned, at Putney Bottom." Putney Bottom was the name given to the area where Beverley Brook crosses the Portsmouth Road where Kingston Vale meets Putney Vale. The actual site of the gibbet was where today Stag Lane joins Roehampton Vale, just prior to the K.L.G. factory.

Today's motorists along the Kingston-Hill–Kingston-Vale stretch of road—and throughout the world—owe much to a family who lived at Aranmor, Kingston Hill, now flats.

They were the Guinness brothers: in particular Kenelm Lee Guinness whose initials form the name of the massive K.L.G. Sparking Plug Factory, Roehampton Vale. This white building with its scarlet-figured clock is a landmark to all using the A3.

A garden workshop may have been the start of this factory, I learn from Mr Charles Allman, of Groveland Way, Malden. Mr Allman, now retired, came to this area in 1916 to work for Mr Nigel Guinness, the youngest of the three brothers.

Algernon (later Sir Algernon) and Kenelm, the elder brothers, were "possibly the finest racing motorists of their time," Mr Allman told me. They were the three sons of Lady Henrietta Guinness, a widow. "I was living in Buckinghamshire and I wanted to be an engineer. I answered an advertisement and came to work for Mr Nigel Guinness who was experimenting with steam engine designs."

Florence Nightingale

On the opposite side of Kingston Hill, and lower down, is Coombe Hurst, now part of the Gipsy Hill section of Kingston Polytechnic. It was at Coombe Hurst that Florence Nightingale passed many happy days as a young woman. It was the home of her favourite Aunt Mai, Mrs Sam Smith. Aunt Mai was the sister of Florence Nightingale's father. She married the younger brother of Florence Nightingale's mother, Fanny.

Owing to the peculiar provisions of the Nightingale property trust, if Florence Nightingale's parents had no son, their considerable wealth and property would pass to the Smiths—as it did. It was inherited in later years by Mr William Shore Smith, the son of Aunt Mai and her husband Sam. It was Shore whom eleven year old Florence called "My boy Shore," when he was laid in her arms, a few days old. Shore's devotion to her and her pride in him became one of the closest ties in her life. Shore's home was Coombe Hurst, too.

Evidence of Florence Nightingale's association with the area is perpetuated today in the name "Florence Terrace," just by Beverley Bridge.

Incidentally, Florence, the younger of the two Nightingale sisters, was so called because she was born in the Italian town of that name. Her elder sister, Parthenope, later Lady Verney, was so named because she was born in Naples, for which this is the Greek name.

It was only after intense opposition from her mother that Florence Nightingale was to find her life's vocation—training nurses. She first tried teaching in a "ragged school" but more and more her thoughts turned to nursing. Aunt Mai proved a staunch supporter and, in 1855, joined Florence Nightingale in her great work at Scutari during the Crimean War.

Later Florence Nightingale quarrelled with Aunt Mai and for nearly twenty years they never met although Uncle Sam and the "Boy Shore" remained in favour.

Coombe Hurst, with its spacious rooms and pleasant grounds, looks today much as it did in Florence Nightingale's youth. She and her sister must have often taken Shore for walks as a child in the attractive walled rose and vegetable garden. Later, aged fourteen, he stayed at the Nightingale's home to convalesce from measles.

There, he was possibly Florence Nightingale's first patient. In a letter she wrote, "While he is with me all that is mine is his, my head and hands and time."

Beverley Bridge

To return to the Kingston boundary area of Kingston Vale, the boundary is formed by Beverley Brook, and the bridge by which the Portsmouth Road crosses the brook is called Beverley Bridge. It bears three remarkable features: a metal plaque and a metal shield proclaiming past "glories" and carved lettering of special significance.

Only two features of the plaque and shield remain accurate today: the name "Beverley Bridge" and the lettering on the top left hand side of the plaque stating "Metropolitan Borough of Wandsworth," if the Greater London Borough can be taken as the Metropolitan Borough. The rest is sadly dated. The top right of the plaque states, "Borough of Malden and Coombe." The bottom left of the shield reads "LCC" and the bottom right says "SCC". Both are now GLC.

The shield and the plaque are on the Malden side of the bridge. On the opposite side, carving in the stonework states: "Bridge built Anno 1754: Enlarged 1776." Beneath is a benchmark sign signifying the bench is a sea-level height-fixing point for ordnance surveys. Besides the bridge is Florence Terrace.

Until comparatively recently, a mounting block used to stand near Beverley Bridge for the benefit of riders. On it was carved the name of Thomas Nuthall, Surveyor of Roehampton, 1654. It also bore this jingle: "From London Town to Portsmouth Downe They Say 'tis miles Three Score."

In the early coaching days, the first and last stop between London and Portsmouth was at Kingston. Towards the close of the coaching period, the horse changes were made shorter and the Robin Hood Inn, Kingston Vale, became the nearest change.

Robin Hood Area

The name Robin Hood, given to the former Robin Hood Farm, Robin Hood Gate and Robin Hood Lane, stems from the Robin Hood games which were a feature of Kingston's medieval life, it is believed. Another theory allies the names to the outlaw who robbed the rich and gave to the poor. Unfortunately, the highwaymen who infested Coombe Woods seemed to believe that charity began at home when it came to sharing out the loot.

Robin Hood Farm ceased to exist about 1937. It had been bisected by the Kingston by-pass and the Kingston Vale housing estate had been built on much of its land. The farmhouse stood in the area at present bounded by Bowness Crescent, Keswick Avenue, part of Robin Hood Lane and the A3.

As a boy, Lord Thurso, who in 1975 donated salmon from his Scottish estates to restock the Thames, lived at Robin Hood Farm. His father was Major Sir Archibald Sinclair. The family lived at the farm from 1923-31.

Robin Hood Farm is mentioned on a map dated 1777, and Lord Thurso's father purchased the farmhouse in 1924 from Colonel Sir Augustus FitzGeorge. It was part of the Earl Spencer's estate of the Manor of Coombe which, in 1837, was incorporated in a deed of conveyance of the Manor to Colonel FitzGeorge's grandfather, Prince Adolphus Frederick, Duke of Cambridge. The last occupant of the farmhouse was a Mr Adrian Pritchard, 1933-7. The farmhouse and the farm seem to have been under separate ownership from 1913 onwards. Aristocratic owners included Major W. Fox Pitt (1913-18) and Lady Sybil de Vere Brassey (1921-2).

The church serving the Kingston Vale area is St John the Baptist, Robin Hood Lane, a little church with a very grand congregation in the 1880s and early twentieth century.

The Duke and Duchess of Teck, parents of Princess Mary (later Queen Mary, wife of George V), lived at White Lodge, Richmond Park. Princess May, as the future Queen was affectionately known, and her fiancé, then Prince of Wales, made their first public appearance following their engagement at a service at St John's Church. Their eldest son, later King Edward VIII (who reigned but was never crowned) was born at White Lodge. An Altar Cross, alone. Thrice the council put up a Bill to Parliament; thrice the Kingston Bill was thrown out.

Disappointed over the consequences to the town when Surbiton secured the railway first, Kingston Council was determined to have its bearing Queen Mary's name, was given to the church by her in memory of her happy days in the Kingston Vale area.

The present church was built in 1861 and later enlarged. Its predecessor was called "Robin Hood Church" and was built as a Chapel-at-Ease for Ham Church (across Richmond Park) in 1839.

The Rev. Dr Biber, headmaster of Coombe House School, off Traps Lane, was the first minister, under the vicar of Ham. This little chapel stood exactly where Robin Hood Lane now joins Kingston Vale. A footpath formed the first approach to later-built St. John's Church and to the church school (now a clinic, library, and general meeting place).

The schools were built in 1856 and, like the two churches, were on the land given by Prince George, Duke of Cambridge. He also paid the £500 needed to build the school and defrayed much of the cost of both churches. When the Chapel-at-Ease was pulled down, the consecrated site was reserved to form the present roadway.

The first vicar of St John's was the Rev. John Aubrey Scott (1849-50). By his time, separation from the parish of Ham had been effected.

Transport in Kingston Borough

It was the tramways which put the finishing touches to Malden's pleasant feeling of village isolation. Until they arrived in the early 1900s, the only road connection with Wimbledon was via Traps Lane and Coombe Lane West. There was, of course, no Kingston by-pass until 1927. The wide area of farmland ruined by the road included the fifty-acre field which has, in part, become Shannon's Corner.

Although this district has a New Malden postmark it is in the borough of Merton, because Beverley Brook, which crosses Burlington Road just prior to Shannon's Corner, is the Kingston borough boundary. It was this brook and its flooding which provided a major headache for tramway executives when they ran the tram lines through to Wimbledon.

I learned of the flood trams that were used to combat water difficulties from Mr Basil J. Pridmore, of Chilmark Gardens, New Malden. Mr Pridmore is a prominent member of the Tramway and Light Railway Society. He is also a leading member of the Light Railway Transport League which studies modern tramways the world over. The flood trams were used near Kingston railway station and in the Wellington Crescent–Kingston Road area of Malden, as well as in the vicinity of Beverley Brook. They were two trams specially converted to provide a shuttle service through the affected areas.

But to return to the actual coming of the trams to Kingston—and to the fight put up by Kingston Council who were determined to go it own trams. The council was, in fact, one of the very few municipal authorities in the country to own its electricity power station. What more natural than that they should desire to own the tramways—and keep all the profits in the town. (The Kingston Corporation Electricity Works had opened on a site adjacent to Down Hall Road in October 1893.)

It was quite certain that Kingston councillors were not intending to allow enterprising engineers from London to provide a tram service, and so battle was joined. I owe the details to a fine book shown me by Mr George Gundry, for many years a West Barnes Lane resident. The book is *London United Tramways: A History, 1894-1933* by Geoffrey Wilson (Allen & Unwin).

Describing Kingston's struggles, Mr Wilson writes, "Tramway promotion was no novelty to Kingston and the first proposals were launched in 1871 by the Kew, Richmond and Kingston Thames Tramways for a line from Richmond to Kingston Market Place. A Bill was thrown out.

"The next attempt, also rejected, came in 1883 when Kingston Corporation and the Surbiton Commissioners jointly promoted quite a comprehensive system. It comprised tramways from Thames Ditton along Portsmouth Road to Kingston Market Place, then via a loop via Fife Road, Kingston Station, Clarence Street. . . .

"In January 1899, the General Purposes Committee of Kingston Corporation threw out proposals by Drake and Gorham for tramways in the area, but decided to call a meeting of all local authorities affected by the schemes. . . . Kingston's Councillor T. Lyne gained support for his view that any tramways ought to be built by the council.

"By June 1899, the Corporation had prepared its own plan. It was a sound enough project, save that most of the lines, except in Clarence and Eden Street, were to be single with loops."

Mr Wilson continues, "Members of the Corporation went to Dover in July and were most impressed by the electric tramways opened there in 1897. They were heartened by a proposal of the London County Council for a light railway from Clapham via Wandsworth and Putney Vale to the county boundary at Beverley Brook, where there was only a $1\frac{1}{4}$-mile gap to the Corporation's projected Kingston Hill terminus." (This was to have been, by the way, at the George and Dragon Inn, Kingston Hill.) "In good hope, the Corporation put forward its Parliamentary Bill on 20 November 1899.

"On 27 March 1900, after two days' consideration, Parliament rejected the Corporation's Bill because it was not comprehensive enough. It is hard to see how a purely municipal scheme could have been more embracing. The Corporation and Civic interests were disappointed and there was a strong feeling that Kingston should try again.

"At the right moment Robinson came forward with a wide-ranging scheme which not only duplicated almost all the Corporation's plans but also extended them to Tolworth, Thames Ditton and Molesey and threw in a branch to Richmond Park Gates."

Kingston Corporation bitterly opposed the ownership of the proposed tramways by the London United Tramways but Surbiton and Malden and Coombe authorities were in favour.

In a last-ditch attempt to own the tramways themselves, in November 1900, "The Tramways Committee of Kingston Corporation," states Mr Wilson, "issued a 14-page statement stressing it was desirable for the Burgesses to retain control of the tramways in the borough.

"Ratepayers met to consider resolutions authorising the Corporation to reapply for tramway powers and oppose the London United Tramways. The meeting overflowed and the proceedings were a series of disorderly interruptions.

"Cllr. Lyne, by this time Chairman of the Tramways Committee, had to sit down half-way through his speech."

Nevertheless, the London United Tramways triumphed and all quarrels were forgotten by 1 March 1906, when the Mayor of Kingston, Cllr. H. C. Minnitt, drove the first tram over Kingston bridge from Hampton Wick. He was assisted by Sir Clifton Robinson, managing director and chief engineer of the London United Tramways.

Kingston was gay with bunting for the occasion. The route on the opening day was to Kingston Hill, back to Surbiton, on to Tolworth and then to Long Ditton and so to Kingston again.

It was almost marred by a tragic accident. On arrival at the George and Dragon Kingston Hill terminus, the Mayor handed over controls to Lewis Bruce, a coloured man who was Sir Clifton's personal driver. As he started down towards Kingston, the tram collided with a Hodgson's Brewery dray mounting the hill. Sir Clifton was knocked from the footplate of the tram and suffered bruises and a sprained ankle. He insisted on continuing the journey—which culminated in a splendid luncheon provided by London United Tramways at Nuthall's Restaurant (now British Home Stores), Thames Street.

Two hundred people sat down to feast. Silk ribbons on the tables represented the tram tracks, slim vases with tulips simulated the trolley poles and lengths of smilax fern the wires. A large wall decoration in daffodils and greenery (the green and yellow colours of the L.U.T.) brought good wishes to the town from the tramway authorities, with the words "Kingston and Tramways United We Stand."

Fig. 19 The Wesleyan Chapel, main road Malden, built 1868.

Fig. 20 Malden Council outing, 1913.

Fig. 21 Marshalling the trams, Eden Street junction, central Kingston.

Fig. 22 A luxury tram, 1906, en route from London Road to Kingston Hill at today's C. & A. corner.

Tramways were open to Malden on 26 May 1906, to Raynes Park on 27 April 1907 and to Wimbledon on 2 May 1907. The Wimbledon authorities, by the way, cost the tramways a fortune: they insisted on the streets being widened at the L.U.T.'s expense.

Tramdrivers of the day were regarded as superbeings by many. They dressed the part. In wet weather they resembled lifeboat coxswain. The cabs were frequently open to the elements and the tramdrivers wore sou'westers in addition to mackintosh capes and leggings.

The actual trams went through disheartening changes. The first trams were luxury vehicles with covered tops. They were found uneconomical to run on the Kingston route. Therefore, after a short time, open top trams were used. These had reversible seats on top and mackintosh aprons were provided for bad weather.

Sir Clifton Robinson, incidentally, lived in Garrick's Villa, Hampton. He had his own personal tram. It called for him each morning. A special tram track went up Sir Clifton's front drive to the door. His death in New York, at the age of sixty-two, was a blow to the British tramcar industry. He had gone to America by invitation to assist in tramcar development. On returning by tramcar from a banquet, he was taken ill and died in a nearby drugstore.

Transport is the key to unity in a borough. After the arrival and demise of the trams it was the turn of the buses to unify Kingston and to promote prosperity. Public transport became established in the order: horse buses, trams, "steamer" buses and similar early types, trolley buses and now pay buses on many routes.

Some older citizens will remember the joys of the gaily painted horse buses. Their main routes radiated from Kingston Market Place.

A popular "run" was to Esher or Richmond. A favourite setting-down place was almost opposite the Shrubsole monument, still a central feature of Kingston Market Place.

London's first horse-drawn "Omnibus," as it was named in capital letters on the coachwork, was used in a service started by George Shillibeer in 1829. His service ran from Paddington Green or Marylebone Road to the Bank. The idea and the name were adopted from a Parisian pioneer Stanislaus Baudry, who gave his vehicles the title "omnibuses," meaning "for all."

Kingston's first horse-buses were spanking affairs, reminiscent of the gay colours of the mail coaches. As with the coaches, extra horses were kept in readiness at local inns to assist uphill. On the horse-bus route from Kingston Market Place via Richmond Road and Ham Common to Richmond, a trace horse was kept in readiness at the Dysart Arms. An extra horse was also put on market wagons coming out of Ham market garden fields on their way to market.

Despite many experiments, the horse-bus was supreme in the London area, including Kingston, until well after 1900. There were actually London horse-buses until 1914. Locally, it was in 1906 that Kingston's first trams arrived. But the horse-buses continued to supplement the services on the Esher and similar routes. Gradually, however, petrol beat hay and the motor-bus took over.

There were some unusual designs but it was the famous B-type bus which made the fortunes of the London General Omnibus Company.

The reign of the tram was long in Kingston, beginning in 1906 and progressing in actual use until the early 1930s, and in the "shadow" well into the mid-1930s, because the outlines of the former tram tracks could be seen in Kingston Road, Malden, and in other places. The rails themselves had been taken up, but the filling in with tarmac showed the outline still.

The buses, to my mind, never attained the dignity of the finest trams. In appearance, the covered trams resembled the stately Mississippi river boats.

The early buses on the Kingston area routes included the famous "steamers." These were buses propelled by steam power and were, in effect, "road locomotives." Paraffin was the fuel often used to fire the steam on a number of buses between the years 1909 and 1919.

By the 1930s experiments were being made with trolley buses. On 21 January 1931, a so-called "Diddler," a new development, was run from Fulwell Depot via Teddington to Kingston Bridge.

It was these "Diddlers" which transformed the Kingston area's road transport. For ten years they reigned supreme in place of the trams. The trolleys were smooth-running, comfortable and regular in timekeeping. The conductors were particularly beloved by schoolchildren as they seemed to have an endless supply of "bus-rolls," the end pieces of their ticket machine rolls, which they saved to give to young passengers.

The end came on 9 May 1962. On that evening, the very last trolley bus in London was run from Wimbledon over the Kingston route to Fulwell Depot. It was trolley bus No. 1521 on route No. 604.

The vehicle was decked with flags and was driven by Mr Albert West, Fulwell Depot's oldest and longest-serving driver. Thousands lined the route. There was sporadic cheering as the bus went past. Crowds sang "Auld Lang Syne" as it drove over the last quarter of a mile to the depot. As many as could climb aboard made short trips on the last journey. Souvenir tickets were issued.

Civic dignatories of the boroughs concerned took part in the farewell. Among them was the Mayor of Malden and Coombe, Councillor William Messenger, of Cambridge Avenue, New Malden.

On the final day of the phased trolley-to-diesel conversion scheme, time from Fulwell and Isleworth depots over seven routes. But the last trolley "home" of all was Kingston's No. 1521 on route 604.

London Transport ran more than a hundred trolley buses for the last

The next day a fleet of Routemaster diesel buses streamed out of Fulwell—among them the No. 281 route Kingston–Malden vehicles.

Kingston By-Pass

The Kingston by-pass was described nationally as Britain's "suicide road," and when the Rt. Hon. Stanley Baldwin M.P., Prime Minister, opened the Kingston by-pass on 28 October 1927, he expressed the hope that adequate facilities would be available to deal with casualties. His foreboding was amply justified: the mounting toll of accidents, many fatal, in the bend near the junction with Coombe Lane West caused the *Sunday Times* to give the road its "death" name in a special article in the 1960s.

Complete reconstruction of the road, including the provision of a dual carriageway, a central crash barrier, pedestrian bridges and overhead intersection roads—including the Ace of Spades and Tolworth underpasses and the latest New Malden underpass—have vastly improved the position.

To return to the serene days of the opening of the by-pass fifty years ago. As the road, one of the first arterial roads in Britain, celebrates its golden jubilee, it is significant to realise that its construction was partly undertaken to ease the unemployment which formed the aftermath of the first world war. The road had first been proposed in 1912.

I have learned details of those road-planning days from former Malden councillor, the late Mr Philip Gooding, elder brother of present Kingston councillor, Mr Kenneth Gooding of Somerset Close, New Malden.

The technical aspects of Kingston by-pass particularly interested Mr Philip Gooding, a cement expert. He became Director of the Cement and Concrete Association and received the O.B.E. and the Honorary Degree of Doctor at Leeds University for his work to increase the technical knowledge of concrete and its uses.

"Traffic in Kingston increased by over 160 per cent between 1913 and 1925," Mr Philip Gooding explained, "The start of the 1914 war delayed the commencement of the Kingston by-pass. Work was begun in 1924. It was then officially known as the Kingston By-Pass and the Merton Connection." The expression "connection" was soon replaced by the word "spur." The main part of the road was eight and a half miles long from Robin Hood Gate (Richmond Park) to Esher, the Merton spur connecting with the Balham and Tooting road. This section was one and a quarter miles. The width of the road throughout was 100 ft between the fences, except at the three bridges over the Southern railway where the road was 60 ft wide. The carriageway was 30 ft wide. In all some 32,000 tons of gravel,

17,000 tons of sand, 8,500 tons of cement and 750 tons of steel were used in constructing the by-pass.

The opening ceremony took place at the spot where the Merton spur joined the main arterial road (now the Merton fly-over). Mr Baldwin cut with scissors a 60 ft white tape suspended across the road from two red Venetian masts. Hundreds watched the ceremony and eight hundred invited guests later took tea in large marquees.

Before the coming of the Kingston by-pass farmland joined the Kingston Vale area to New Malden. Only a few grand houses, Robin Hood Farm and a handful of cottages formed the Kingston Vale habitations. The present modern house development came later. Fortunately, the provision of sports grounds on either side of the road prevented the ribbon development which is a feature of sections of the road through New Malden and Tolworth. The 1935 *Ribbon Development Act* came too late to prevent this building, occasioned because builders took advantage of sites with easy access. They cashed in on the fact that, in the early 1930s, buyers would pay extra for a main-road site.

It was the public-spiritedness of a Kingston Vale man which set the rural pattern of this first section of the by-pass. He was Mr Richardson Evans who led a campaign to keep both banks of Beverley Brook free from building.

As a tribute to his work the Richardson Evans Memorial Playing Fields (forty-two acres) were opened in July 1931 by the chairman of the London Playing Fields Association. The handsome pavilion, the lands and the Cross of Remembrance in a grove of oak trees were paid for by public subscription. The public are welcome to use the café in the pavilion up to 5 p.m. It has a large car park and is just prior to Beverley Bridge, Roehampton Lane.

The massive granite memorial cross, ornamented with a drawn sword in polished granite, stands on a plinth formed by three steps and is set on a granite dais. A five-acre circle of oak trees surrounds the Cross. It is very well worth seeing and is at the far side of the playing fields.

On the base of the Cross are these inscriptions: "The land around—42 acres—is dedicated to public use in the memory of all those who having been resident or belonging to families resident in the adjoining districts gave their lives in the Great War, 1914-1918."

The other inscription reads: "Nature provides the best monument. This perfecting the work must be left to the gentle hand of time but each returning spring will bring a fresh tribute to those whom it is desired to keep in everlasting remembrance."

A regular payment towards maintenance of Wimbledon Common is paid through their rates by all Kingston citizens living within three-quarters of a mile of the Common. This money is paid to Kingston Borough Council and is then passed on to the Wimbledon and Putney Common Conservators. This body was set up by Act of Parliament in 1871 when the Earl Spencer, owner of the Commons, offered them for sale.

Today, the body of Conservators which administers the Commons is constituted exactly as when the Act was passed. They are eight in number. Five Conservators are elected. The other three are nominated respectively by the Home Secretary, Minister of Defence and Secretary of State for the Environment.

Nonsuch Palace

As described earlier, until 1938 the vicars of St John the Baptist, Old Malden, were also vicars of St Mary the Virgin, Chessington, and the parish title was Malden-cum-Chessington. This tangled history is a result of Walter de Merton's legacy of the area to Merton College, Oxford.

In 1975 a joint party from the two churches visited Merton College to study old records as part of the centenary celebrations commemorating the enlargement of St. John's in 1875.

Centenary celebrations can result in the revelation of extraordinary facts. Few can be more strange than a bizarre bargain struck by Queen Elizabeth I which resulted in the "swopping" of Malden and Chessington for the Tudor royal Palace of Nonsuch, famed throughout Europe for its splendour and magnificence.

I learned about this transaction from Mr Rowley Hall, of Brockenhurst Avenue, historian and churchwarden of St John the Baptist, Old Malden.

In 1578, Queen Elizabeth I procured from Merton College, Oxford, owners of the Manor of Malden (which included Chessington) a 5,000-year lease of Malden Manor and the right and responsibility of presenting a vicar of St John's (who also was vicar of St Mary's) and of the church expenses. For this lease, she agreed to pay an annual rent of £40 a year.

But the Queen did not want Malden and Chessington for state property, she wished to recover ownership of the nearby Tudor Palace of Nonsuch, built by King Henry VIII.

Nonsuch was built on the site of the former village of Cuddington and remains of its banqueting hall were excavated some years ago just off the road to Epsom past the Organ Inn, Ewell, by the late John Dent and helpers. A plaque commemorating the unearthing of the foundations can be seen there today. To preserve the foundations, they were covered with earth again after careful mapping. Before this was done, the site was displayed for a summer to the public and was visited by hundreds of sightseers.

"The granting of the lease to Queen Elizabeth was quite extraordinary and almost unbelievable," Mr Hall said. "There is no doubt about the event. The reason is more obscure. According to the county histories of the eighteenth and nineteenth century, Queen Elizabeth wished to recover the estate and Palace of Nonsuch which had been purchased in the reign of Queen Mary by the Earl of Arundel." Although details are obscure, it appears that Queen Elizabeth forced Merton College, Oxford, to countenance the exchange of her 5,000-year lease of Malden Manor with the Earl of Arundel for Nonsuch Palace.

"St John's Church was so badly neglected as a result of this transaction that in 1596 Queen Elizabeth was petitioned by Malden villagers to help repair their 'now decayed' church. It was not until 1627 that Merton College revoked the 5,000 year lease."

Ill fortune still befell the church fabric. The tower nearly fell down in 1770. During the depression and rural discontent after the Battle of Waterloo the deterioration continued unchecked until 1844 and 1847 when emergency steps were taken.

It was the forty-four year ministry of the Rev. William Chetwynd Stapylton, starting in 1850, which rescued St John's. The church was repaired in 1863, enlarged in 1867 and again in 1875, the reason for the 1975 centenary celebrations.

Queen Elizabeth spent considerable time at Nonsuch Palace, but after her reign its fortunes steadily declined. King Charles II gave it to his favourite, Barbara Villiers, Duchess of Cleveland, and she sold it to pay her bills.

Cuddington

The borough boundaries between Kingston, Sutton and Merton today split the Worcester Park area into three. Parishioners at St Mary's Church, Cuddington (at the top of The Avenue, Worcester Park), come from three boroughs.

Until comparatively recently the large church seemed isolated. It was built by the leaders of the local population in 1867 when building development was beginning to creep up the hill after the arrival of the railway.

For four centuries the name Cuddington had no real meaning. The village bearing that name and its church had been razed to the ground by King Henry VIII to make way for his Nonsuch Palace. To add to the tangle, most of the original Cuddington parish, including the site of the first St Mary the Virgin, is not now in the parish of the present church.

Only a year after the new church was built, the parishes of St Philip (Worcester Park), St John the Baptist (Stoneleigh) and St Francis' (Ruxley Lane) were carved out of the once-large parish.

The St Mary's centenary was celebrated with a number of special events in 1967. Among them was a memorable performance of T. S. Eliot's *Murder in the Cathedral* staged by the Cuddington Players.

At present, the church stands in the centre of a triangle of roads. One of these is an unmade-up road called "Royal Avenue." This leads to the precipitous Barrow Hill and on to Worcester Park Road, Kingston Road and via Surbiton, towards the river and Hampton Court Palace.

Worcester Park

King Edward VII was a frequent visitor to "Mount Tavey," a house where The Avenue meets Cleveland Road. There was plenty of rough shooting in the area—and the King was a famous "gun." All this land once formed part of the Nonsuch Palace estate.

The Earl of Worcester was appointed Keeper of the Nonsuch Palace 911-acre "Great Park"—hence the present name Worcester Park.

The Earl built a "Great Lodge" to overlook his domain. It appears to have been completed during 1601.

Near the Earl's "Great Lodge" at the top of today's "The Avenue" was a Keeper's Lodge, a two-storey timbered house. It was this smaller house, I understand, which became Worcester Park Farmhouse, lodging of some eminent Pre-Raphaelite artists.

Worcester Park's Artistic Life

Some of Britain's most famous paintings were painted in the Old Malden and Worcester Park area.

Worcester Park Farmhouse, The Avenue, was the home of the Pre-Raphaelites: the group of artists who included Sir John Millais (born in Kingston), Holman Hunt, Ford Madox Brown and Dante Gabriel Rossetti. They lived a community life, devoting themselves to art in the years around 1852.

The muse of their creation was Elizabeth Siddal. She modelled Ophelia for Millais in his masterpiece which now is hung in the Tate Gallery. For this painting she was not required actually to lie in the Hogsmill—only the background of that river was painted from life (possibly off Church Road near Worcester Park House); however, she had to lie for hours in a bath of water at Millais' London studio. The bath was heated by candles, but these usually burnt out before Millais finished working, and Elizabeth caught the cold which is thought to have finally turned to the tuberculosis from which she died, in 1862 at the age of 28. She married Rossetti and inspired some of his finest work.

Another great picture painted locally by Millais was "A Huguenot Refusing to Shield Himself from Danger by Wearing a Roman Catholic Badge." This almost photographic painting shows an incident during the St Bartholomew's Day Massacre in 1572 when numbers of French Huguenots were slaughtered by order of Catherine de Medici. "The Hireling" (now in Manchester Art Gallery) was painted in the countryside between Surbiton and Ewell.

It was while living at Worcester Park Farmhouse (at the top of The Avenue) that Holman Hunt painted "The Light of the World," depicting Christ knocking at a door, long thought to be the door of St John the Baptist Church. Hunt wrote: "My further steps led me into a path at the side of the stream. Between me and the water was a hut long since abandoned by the powder workers. With my new picture in view I had special reasons for wishing to see the further side by night, and walked through the thick grass to explore it. On the river side was a door locked up and overgrown with tendrils of ivy, its step choked with weeds."

The ghostly trees in the background of "The Light of the World" were painted in moonlight in the garden of Worcester Park Farm. Hunt used a specially-built "hide" as his studio.

Painters were wealthy men in Victorian days, if successful. Hunt was paid a fortune for his two "Light of the World" paintings. They are almost identical, only the character of the weeds at the foot of the door varies. One painting hangs in Keble College, Oxford. The other is in St Paul's Cathedral, London. When Hunt died, he left £163,000, painting having been his sole source of livelihood since the age of sixteen.

Similarly, Millais, who lived in Portsmouth Road, Kingston, as a lad, received a knighthood for his prowess. At the height of his fame, he earned between £20,000 and £40,000 a year—at a time when such money had real value.

In their day, these artists were the avant-garde of British art. Many contemporary critics decried their work; others praised their imaginative realism and almost miraculous presentation of detail.

Famous writers as well as painters lived at Worcester Park. They were H. G. Wells and the renowned Victorian writer, Mrs Alexander Hector.

A rather unflattering picture of Worcester Park is given by H. G. Wells in *Ann Veronica,* published in 1909. Wells lived at 41 The Avenue (now a modern housing development) from 1896-7. The area Morningside Park in his novel is in reality Worcester Park.

He described the place as "a suburb that had not altogether, as people say, come off. . . . There was first The Avenue, which ran in a consciously elegant curve from the railway station into an undeveloped wilderness of agriculture, with big yellow brick villas on either side, and then there was the Pavement, the little clump of shops about the post office, and under the railway arch was a congestion of workmen's dwellings."

Some of the "big yellow villas" still remain in The Avenue. The Pavement, its little clump of shops and the post office (latterly a business premises beside the present Worcester Hotel) have been redeveloped into handsome office premises with modern shops.

The other famous author was a long-established resident of Worcester Park. She wrote about forty successful Victorian novels, some going to three volumes in the manner of the times, under the pen-name Mrs Alexander, taking her husband's Christian name for her writing. Their home was the splendid mansion first called Worcester House and later Worcester Court.

Its massive brick garden wall, at the junction of The Avenue and Delta Road is, I believe, the back-ground of Sir John Millais' Huguenot masterpiece.

Mrs Alexander Hector was a prolific writer until late in life, despite a fairly large family. Her titles include *Which Shall It Be?* and *Her Dearest Foe*. In a book of short stories, she shared the honours with Thomas Hardy and the Marquis of Lorne.

Men of letters visited the house and her eldest daughter, Ida, was Sir Henry Rider Haggard's only secretary for thirty-five years.

After Mrs Hector's death around 1904 the house was let for a long time and finally sold. Eventually, it became Blakesley House school until around 1950. It was sold for building, but the wall remains.

Worcester Park Station and Malden Green

Several Acts of Parliament were needed to safeguard Malden Green Common rights and a special Act, passed in 1871, enabled the developers of the Great Avenue (now The Avenue), Worcester Park, to gain proper access for their clients to the trains.

A determined and persevering man— Mr James W. Johnson, town clerk in 1941 to the then Borough of Malden and Coombe—has put the facts on record in his report *Malden Green Commons, a history and record of local events dating from* 1841 *to* 1941.

The Malden Green controversy, possibly simmering for years, flared up with the coming of the railway to the area following the *Epsom and Leatherhead Railway Act,* 1856, and the *Wimbledon and Dorking Railway Act,* 1857.

Officials concerned with the events leading to the building of Worcester Park station (originally "Old Malden for Worcester Park"), were the Masters and Fellows of Merton College, Oxford (Lords of the Manor), the Surveyor of Highways (Thomas Dring, Plough Inn,

Malden) and the parish clerk, Thomas Lock, Malden.

It was easy enough to build the railway station—getting to it with ease was the difficulty. Unauthorised encroachments on Malden Green Common Land, the tenacity of a local land-owner Mr Thomas Weeding (now buried in a magnificent tomb in the churchyard of St John the Baptist, Old Malden) and the desires of property developers clashed with such violence that Parliament passed *The Worcester Park Road Extension Act,* 1871, a private members bill initiated by the Landed Estates Company Ltd. of Worcester Park, developers of The Avenue.

By a deed dated 14 May 1870, Merton College authorities (Lords of the Manor), granted the Landed Estates Company (developers of The Avenue) the right of way over a small piece of Malden Green Common.

The company made a road over this land and, shortly afterwards, litigation took place between the company and Mr Thomas Weeding. He claimed to have rights as a commoner and proceeded to break up the road.

As a result, the 1871 Act was passed, and the access road from the railway station to The Avenue was laid out as it is today.

Further struggles however, lay ahead. The small piece of common land bordering the new access road was supposed to be planted to shrubs and kept attractive by the Landed Estate Company. It, however, went into liquidation and the land became bedraggled and rubbish-strewn.

The redoubtable vicar of St. John the Baptist, Old Malden, the Rev. Chetwynd Stapylton, took matters in hand. He offered Merton College, Oxford, a token rent of 1s. annually for the right to "take charge of, repair the fences and keep the ground tidy" of a small piece of common land which had been annexed as part of the garden of a house called Elm Lodge. This 1s. rent was paid for years by St John's vestry and was finally taken over by Malden and Coombe Borough Council.

This peaceful conclusion was not reached without a fight. A Mr Alan Wood, a local butcher, was appointed by the Maldens and Coombe Urban District Council to be a responsible ranger for the land.

Regretfully, reports Mr Johnson, he began to regard the land as "an important part of his adjoining freehold and the land was not only being used as a shrubbery and place of rest but was being appropriated extensively as a petrol and business dump and a convenient rustic shelter as a retreat from the business premises" (a butcher's shop).

"Statutory notice was served upon the ranger to quit his office of responsibility and to remove his possessions from the land," states Mr Johnson.

"He refused and took every possible measure to be obstructive, even to threatening violence to the Clerk of the Council and his followers. The Engineer and Surveyor (Mr R. H. Jeffes), was consulted and informed that there was a pending battle for the exercise of public rights and anything might be expected in expelling an old friend from his concealed effort to gain a prescriptive right, viz, 'a valuable corner site.'

"It was agreed to employ a strong contingent of the highway staff under the direction of Mr Empson, Road Foreman, to enter upon the land, again giving Mr Wood, the butcher, full opportunity of complying with the orders of the council.

"Pugilistic scenes took place outside his establishment, and the noble workmen, with skill and judgement, steadily removed the rustic shelter of historic fame in the old parish to a highway lorry and proceeded, in warrior fashion, to Mr Wood's farm away up on Cheam Hill where the gates were found to be padlocked, and again a fiery ordeal aroused public attention."

The boundary fences of the corner site were then removed and with ceremonial effect the Common Land was finally and systematically posted under the Confirmation Scheme. The incident, states Mr Johnson, although peculiarly interesting, was generally regretted by the officers of the local authority in view of the family interests and friendship in the ancient parish. The Act of Enforcement was commenced and completed on Thursday, 27 August 1925.

"Mr Alan Wood was buried at Malden parish church. The date of his death, recorded on his tombstone in the churchyard, is 22 September 1925."

Those people living in the Old Malden area will find a good deal of interest in the lands belonging to Thomas Weeding which were enfranchised at Court Baron on 8 August 1856. Enfranchised means in this case setting free from manorial rights; Court Baron is an assembly of the freehold tenants under the presidency of the Lord of the Manor or his High Steward.

The lands concerned cost £800 for tithe enfranchisement "fine," £70 for "quit rents," £450 for timber and various other payments totalled in all £1,388 11s. 3d.—a very considerable sum in 1856. However, bearing in mind the extensive housing development on the lands, Merton College did not get a very good price.

Weeding's lands involved included "Shoulder of Mutton Field," "Highdown Field," "Cos's Acres," "Great Hollands," "Fullbrooks," "Little Andrews," "Oak Tree Mead," "Ley's Six Acres," "Meadow Hill," "Old Sarah's Field" and part of "High Ditches."

The names recall the time when Sow Lane was the name for today's South Lane, New Malden, and the Kingston by-pass was an unheard-of development. Carriages and horse-drawn carts were the only wheeled vehicles to traverse the often-rutted lanes.

Flocks of sheep or cattle were still herded to market. The way of life for many cottagers had changed little over the centuries.

The original St Mary the Virgin, Cuddington, was in the lost village from the twelfth century until its destruction in 1538. The builders of today's St Mary the Virgin, Cuddington, felt the name should not be lost, with its historic link with Walter de Merton, St Mary's vicar in 1284 and the founder of Merton College, Oxford.

Their new church was built almost on the boundary of the former Cuddington parish, reconstituted legally by the Ecclesiastical Commissioners in 1896.

The parish hall of the new St Mary the Virgin was built on the Malden Road and was, until the mid-1930s at least, still called the Cuddington Institute. It was later named The Institute and is now the parish hall of St John the Baptist, Old Malden.

Worcester Park, Malden, has been the product of the railway. Even the coaching route from London via Coombe Hill, New Malden, and on to Old Malden for Epsom did not go to Worcester Park, but passed on to Ewell via Church Road and Worcester Park Road, turning off Malden Road at Plough Green.

This four-in-hand coach was running regularly within living memory. Mr Jack Mills, a retired postman now living in Washington Road, Worcester Park, used to walk to New Malden from Old Malden as a boy to get butter from the Maypole shop. He used to "hitch" a lift on the coach back to Old Malden on his way home.

The Headquarters of the Worcester Park Hunt (the noted Beagle Pack) used to be at the inn by Worcester Park station. Its name "Huntsman's Hall" derives from the Hunt, established in 1886. The beagles were kept in kennels in Green Lane.

As surburbia encroached on country, the dogs were merged with the North Sussex and Surrey Beagles and housed at Wild Acres, Ifield Wood, near Crawley. They gave a convincing demonstration of skill several years ago at the Surrey County Show, Guildford.

The Worcester Park railway station forecourt is almost exactly the same today as over a hundred years ago. It then offered spacious accommodation for carriages. There were some fine houses for the gentry in and around old Worcester Park. These included "Fullbrooks" (from which Fullbrooks Avenue takes its name).

Strange now-vanished names graced some of the area. Hunters Hill was the title of today's Barrow Hill, now being developed off Church Road, Mount Tavey was the old name for Worcester Park's Cleveland Road. Today's Salisbury Road and Cuddington Avenue were once a track called "Curly Dog Tail" leading to a brickfield, now built over, an area comprising Stoneleigh Park Road, Ardrossan Gardens and Wolsey Close.

The early name for today's Central Road, Worcester Park, was Cheamside. At the top of the hill, leading up from the Victorian railway station, was picturesque Thorn Cottage. The middle of the road formed the boundary between the parishes of Cheam and Cuddington.

Cheam parish authorities were far-sighted enough to install street lighting, but Cuddington parish refused. In Cheamside, at the junction with Longfellow Road, was a little row of ten shops, including the baker's premises, still there today.

The first building development in the area was in Longfellow Road in 1865 and the next forty years saw great strides in development. More houses were actually built than were required and rents seldom exceeded seven shillings a week. Longfellow Road and Washington Road were the "pioneer" streets.

Characters of the time included Miss Rose Emma Smith, born in 1849 in an imposing house called "The Oaks" in The Avenue, Worcester Park. When her parents died, she took up residence in Washington Road to be near the children she taught in the Sunday school.

Under her auspices, literally hundreds of London Sunday school children came down to Worcester Park each summer for a fortnight's holiday in the country. They stayed with local people. Once a year, Miss Smith organised the annual Sunday school treat to Worthing, at an inclusive fee of 2s. 6d.

When Miss Smith died in 1927 at the age of 78, a memorial tablet in her honour was placed in St Philip's Church. Her lifetime had seen the emergence of Worcester Park from a huddle of houses to an embryo town. In her young days, boys used to play cricket down the middle of what is now Central Road, the main shopping and bus route.

The station area was famed in 1906 for another sport—shooting. It was the venue of the "Wimbledon Shooting Grounds," sixty acres in extent and admirably laid out for practice in any form of modern shooting, according to *The County Gentlemen*, journal of the day. The management was in the "extremely capable hands of Mr Claude Brooking, one of the most skilful and experienced shooting coaches in England."

Pheasant shooting was provided from towers, 65 ft, 85 ft and 105 ft in height. The shooting grounds provided the most realistic representation of partridge driving over natural fences and grouse driving over real butts.

Charges were 7s. 6d. for practice and attendance, cartridges 8s. 4d. for 100 and clay birds 8s. 4d. per 100. Live birds were also available.

Memories of Worcester Park

How Worcester Park grew, as seen by her citizens, has produced a harvest of memories.

Here are some reminiscences of trudging miles to school, the delights of country walks, country pursuits and of a real village life where cricket was played in the middle of what is now the busy Central Road, a main thoroughfare between Malden, Cheam and Sutton.

In the 1900s, this now major road was called Cheamside. It was a "dirt" road with cottages and two farms. There was a cluster of shops near the station. Of these, Morley's the bakers is the only one to survive in the same family and with the same facade.

Mr Peter Kinton, Kingston's Director of Personal Services, and his twin brother Ronald, knew Worcester Park well before the immense changes which came about through the middle 1930s housing development. This linked the area with Morden and stretched the village in a "ribbon" development all the way to Sutton.

Scouting in Worcester Park and the area owes much to the Kinton twins. Today, Mr Peter Kinton is Group Scout leader of the 4th Worcester Park Scout Group. His wife, Sheila, leads one of the three Cub-Scout packs in the group.

The Balmoral Road heaquarters is called "Appeldoorn" because the group is linked with Scouts in Appeldoorn, Holland. Ronald Kinton is District Commissioner for Scouts in Sutton and Cheam.

"It was in 1929 that my parents moved to Worcester Park from London," said Mr Kinton. "Those days were just before the vast house-building expansion which resulted from the London tube train extension to Morden.

"One of the flourishing societies of the time was the Worcester Park Horticulture Society of which my father, Walter Kinton, was secretary."

"My brother and I joined the 2nd Worcester Park Scouts—and scouting has become a life-long interest to us both. In the days when we were lads, we camped in the fields of the area which is now Stoneleigh and is completely built over. In those days, money was scarcer and transport was not so easily arranged. We held our camps on local sites."

Closely associated with the growth of scouting in Worcester Park over the years was Mr Leslie Fancourt of Cheam Common Road, until recently Group Scout Leader of the 1st Cuddington Sea Scout Group.

He joined the 1st Worcester Park Group as an eight year old in 1918. He joined the 2nd Worcester Park Group in 1921 and took up leadership of that Group around 1930. As a boy chorister, he joined St Philip's church choir in 1918 in the time of the Rev. R. B. Ravenscroft. In 1920, he went to Tiffin Boys School, Kingston, then in the Fairfield building which is now St Joseph's Roman Catholic school.

"As small boys, we used to walk across the fields from behind the Worcester Hotel to the Hogsmill River to swim in the stream," he said. "The only bus service locally in those days was along the London Road from Clapham to Dorking. We used to cycle to school in Kingston. It was a country ride."

A man whose family business did much to create Worcester Park as it is today is Mr Leslie Young, secretary for fifteen years of the Worcester Park Chamber of Trade. His father, George William Young founded G. W. Young (Builders) Ltd., 64 Central Road, in 1908. Among the roads of houses the firm built are Kingsmead Avenue, Brinkley Road and the Browning Avenue estates

Looking back, Mr Leslie Young recalled seeing 1914-18 prisoners of war with their pill-box hats, working in the fields near Worcester Park railway station. Steam trains ran at two-hourly intervals via Worcester Park to London when he was a schoolboy going to Blakesley House School, then at Merton and later at the top of The Avenue, Worcester Park. If he missed the train, it was a three to four mile walk.

Doctors were the first people in the area to have cars. The "gentry" had carriages, the rest had ponies and traps, or bicycled or walked.

The first "village" policeman in Worcester Park was Mr Ernest White, father of Mr Sidney White, Cheam Common Road.

"Dad joined the police on 12 September 1898," said Mr White. "He served until 16 September 1924, with 'exemplary conduct.' He was stationed at Battersea as a young man. One day an inspector said to him: 'You're a countryman'—he came from Wiltshire—'we want someone to go to a little place in the suburbs called Worcester Park to see about chicken thieves there.'

"Dad went—and stayed for twenty-six years in the police. He died in 1954, having served in the Home Guard during the last war as the oldest private in his Company. My brother, Herbert, and I served with the National Fire Service.

"I served at the Forge Garage, Central Road, then the war-time fire station. On duty, the firemen lived in flats over the adjoining shops. My brother Herbert was at the fire station at the White Cross Garage, Sutton by-pass. Dad's Home Guard unit was at the Columbia Sports Ground, Motspur Park, Malden, now the B.B.C. ground. Our eldest brother, Ernest, was in the R.A.F.

"Our family used to live at 243 Cheam Common Road, a country cottage (now a shop). As lads, we could walk for miles in real countryside. Worcester Park Cricket Club," he added, "was originally at the rear of Cheam Common Road. They had a piece of ground belonging to Blake's farm. Their present ground is beside Beverley Brook near Worcester Park station."

A man who has had a "front seat" throughout the development of Worcester Park is Mr John William Morley, master baker of Central

Road. There has been a baker's shop on the site for a hundred years. Mr Morley's father bought the shop in 1909.

Although entirely modernised, the upper facade looks much the same today as it did about seventy years ago. Then the family "lived in." Now, the business takes all the premises.

"There was plenty to do in the old days," said Mr Morley. "The Worcester Park United Cycling Club was founded in 1907. Dad was a member and practically all the boys in the village belonged. I first went to Cheam Common Infants School, Balmoral Road and then to Burlington Junior School in New Malden. I used to walk to school in Malden but sometimes got a lift home.

"We used to see cattle being driven down Green Lane, Worcester Park, and on to Kingston cattle market through New Malden. They used to drink at the Malden Fountain.

"I started work very young. At twelve, I used to help my father and before long was working full time. The flour for the bread we made used, at one time, to be ground at a water mill at Ewell. Then it came from London by horse and cart. It was a day's work for the miller's delivery men. Now it comes by lorry in paper sacks. In the old days there were as many as twelve grades of flour used for the different types of baking. Now there are only two. These two types are known as 'straight-run' for breadmaking and 'patents' for cakes.

"Kids still like doughnuts but the once farthing buns are now $3\frac{1}{2}$p or 4p. One of our early special orders was the once-a-year Christmas party batch of buns for Pastor Baldwin at his church hall. He always specified four currants to a bun.

"Every Friday I used to travel up to the Elephant and Castle, London, to fetch home the shop's crumpet supplies. I walked to the Elephant and Castle from Waterloo. My fare to London was $10\frac{1}{2}d$. return.

"On Sundays a crumpet man used to go round the streets locally with a tray on his head, ringing a bell to attract customers. We bought what he did not sell and sold them next day.

"A memory of those old days can be seen on the collection plate of the pillar box in Windsor Road, a turning off Central Road. This plate bears the name 'Cheamside Collection,' dating from when it used to be at the junction of Longfellow Road and Cheamside Road, now Central Road. When the road was widened, the pillar box was shifted to Caldbeck Avenue, higher up the hill. Now it has gone across Central Road to Windsor Road."

All three of the Morley boys became bakers. John took over his father's shop. Frank went to Toronto, Canada, and the other brother, Geoffrey, is in business in Rochester, Kent.

Two heirloom sets of trade measures are the cherished property of Mr Stanley Pearson who recently retired after fifty-three years in the business: first in New Malden and, since 1924, in Worcester

Fig. 23. The flood trams, Burlington Road.

Fig. 24 Cheamside, Worcester Park, now Central Road.

Park. One of the sets, in wood and brass, belonged to his father, Mr James Charles Pearson.

Originally a wholesale corn merchant in London, his father entered the retail trade in January 1915, by purchasing a corn chandler's at No. 13 Coombe Road, now the site of A. R. Hill and Son, shoe retailers. Selling seeds and all manner of fertilisers, including Canary Guano, Mr Pearson was also a coal merchant.

The business took on plants and other items of nursery trade as the result of a lucky encounter between young Stanley Pearson, then a lad in his first year in business, and Lord Ripon's head gardener at Coombe Court, the former Galsworthy house in George Road, Coombe Hill.

The gardener, Mr Smith, asked Stanley if he would like some spare phlox plants for sale. Stanley jumped at the chance—and branched out on his own in the business, starting a plant section.

Incidentally, he had been delivering five tons of coke and 2,000 bundles of wood to Coombe Court—"quite a usual order."

In 1924, when the lease on the Malden shop had two years left to run, Mr James Pearson purchased the business of Waites, corn chandlers and seedsmen, Worcester Park. It had previously been Webb and Thompson and earlier still Penningtons. At that time, the business was on the same side of the road as Morley's the bakers. In 1923, the address became 1 Cheamside. This was changed to 328 Cheam Common Road, then to 146 Central Road, and now to 157 Central Road. Besides changing addresses, the shop moved across the road to its present site.

Violent thunderstorms in August and annual flooding of Beverley Brook in the dip down by Worcester Park railway station are vivid memories of Mr Pearson's days in business with his father. Mr Pearson senior died on 23 August 1941. Stanley Pearson was his eldest son. There were nine in the family.

And Now

In this year, 1977, the Silver Jubilee anniversary of Queen Elizabeth II's accession to the throne, the Royal Borough of Kingston upon Thames is an amalgamation of the three boroughs of Kingston, Surbiton and of Malden and Coombe. The present Royal Borough resulted from the creation of the Greater London Council in 1964-5.

The challenge of the times has been met resolutely in the past twelve years by the new Kingston borough and its near neighbours. The next twenty-five will see consolidation of progress and a vital leap forward in prosperity.

The Royal Borough's gift to the Queen from her citizens is to be a £5,000 fund to enable Silver Jubilee trees to be planted at sites throughout the borough.

Tree No. 1, a silver birch, was planted in January at Surbiton Lagoon by Kingston's No. 1 citizen, Princess Alexandra, who lives within the borough boundaries at Thatched House, Richmond Park. Tree No. 2 was planted at the Lagoon by the Mayor, Councillor Frank Steptoe, and tree No. 3 was planted there by Mr L. E. Rowan Bentall. A further twenty-two silver birches were then planted at the Lagoon by council workmen.

The tree scheme was initiated the preceding year by the then Mayor, Councillor Frank Gaisford. All donors of £10 to the tree scheme receive a handsome Silver Jubilee presentation picture of a tree. A book of donors' names will be presented to the Queen.

Thus, in planting for the future, in an historic pageant at Kingston parish church, All Saints, and in street parties for children in Jubilee fetes, processions and firework displays, 1977 will be a high spot for ever in Kingston's history.

Evans, Richardson, 88
Ewell Road, 25, 30, 31, 35, 37

Fairfield, The, 1, 2, 6, 7, 20, 21, 22
Fairfield, The, 2, 3, 7, 8, 21, 22, 23
Farouk, King, 27, 77, 78
Fife Road, 6, 16, 17
Finny, Dr W. E. St Lawrence, 2, 24
Fireball Alley, 31
Fisher, Sir Nigel, 42
Fishponds, 33, 35
Fitzgeorge Avenue, 62, 63
Fitzgeorge School, 62
Fitzgerald, Lady Edward, 39, 40
Foley, Lord, 40
Forsyte Saga, The, 63, 64
Fountain Court, 8
Fountain Hotel, 54
Free Church of England, 51
Friends Meeting House, 10
Fullers Way North, 37

Gaisford, Councillor Frank, 102
Galitzine, Prince Vladimir, 43
Galsworthy, John, 63, 64, 75
Galsworthy Road, 48, 63
Garrison Lane, 42, 43, 44
Gent, Lionel, 62, 66
George and Dragon, The, 83, 84
George V, 77, 81
George VI, 15, 23
George, Duke of Cambridge, 3, 22, 47, 49, 53, 56, 59, 62, 66, 67, 77, 82
George Street, 29
Gipsy Hill, Kingston Polytechnic, 76, 77, 78
Glenbuck Road, 36
Gloucester Road, 63
Gooding, Councillor Kenneth, 87
Gooding, Philip, 87
Gosbury Hall, 41
Gosbury Hill, 41
Grafton Road, 53, 58, 62
Graham Spicer Institute, 50, 51, 52, 53
Great Lodge, 91
Green Lane, 97
Griffin Hotel, 4, 7
Grist, Charles J., 22
Groves, The, 58, 59, 60

Guildhall, Kingston, 2, 4
Guilford Avenue, 26

Hall, Rowley, 89
Hall, Rowley, 90
Ham, 24, 85
Hammond, Robert, 10
Hampton Court Palace, 1, 3, 12, 22, 34, 39, 45, 91
Hare, Thomas and Eleanor, 41
Harrow Passage, 6
Hawker, Harry George, 19, 41
Hawker Siddeley Aviation Ltd., 18, 19, 20, 41
Hawks Passage, 13
Hawks Road, 47
Heathen Street, 9, 48
Hector, Mrs Alexander, 92, 93
Henry VIII, 3, 12, 23, 42, 45, 65, 68, 90
High Street (Kingston), 1, 2, 28
High Street (Malden), 50, 52, 53
Hillcroft College, 35, 36
Hodgson's Brewery, 7, 84
Hogsmill River, 2, 21, 44, 46, 91, 99
Hogsmill Watersplash, 7
Hollyfield Road, 33
Hollyfield School, 33
Holy Cross Convent, 50
Holy Trinity Church, 51, 53
Home of Compassion, 39
Homersham, Councillor Alfred, 14, 21
Homersham Road, 14
Hook Road, 41
Hook War Memorial, 41
Hopping Wood, 71
Hoppingwood Avenue, 71
Hunt, Holman, 91, 92
Hunt, Monsignor Hugh, 49

Imber Court, 40

Jefferies, Richard, 35
Jefferies Wood, 35
Jerome, Jerome K., 22
Johnson, James W., 93, 94, 95
Jubilee Fountain, 21
Jubilee Tree Fund, 24, 102

Kavanagh, Steven, 37
Keiller, Mrs Gabrielle, 73
Kenry House, 77, 78
Keswick Avenue, 81
King Charles Road, 33
King's Avenue, 53
King's Passage, 8
King's Road, 23
Kingston and Long Grove Hospital Group, 31
Kingston and Richmond Area Health Authority, 31
Kingston Barracks, 27, 69
Kingston Borough Central Parks Nursery, 45
Kingston Bridge, 1, 2, 10, 11, 14, 67, 74
Kingston By-pass, 87, 88
Kingston College of Further Education, 7, 8, 17
Kingston Corporation Baths, 14
Kingston Corporation Electricity Works, 23, 83
Kingston Grammar School, 4, 12, 13, 16, 28, 47
Kingston Hill, 63, 74, 75, 76, 77
Kingston Hill Place, 76, 77
Kingston Hospital, 48
Kingston Library and Museum, 1, 2, 9, 20, 46
Kingston markets, 6, 41
Kingston Police Station, 2
Kingston Post Office, 6, 7
Kingston Railway Station, 13, 14, 15, 22, 53
Kingston Road (Kingston), 48, 49, 59, 62, 86
Kingston Road (Tolworth), 45, 91
Kingston Roller Skating Rink, 17
Kingston, Surbiton and District Fire Brigade, 5, 13
Kingston tannery, 10
Kingston Vale, 53, 66, 77, 78, 79
Kingston War Memorial, 14, 16
Kinton, Peter, 98, 99

Ladderstile Gate, 71, 72
Langley Avenue, 29
Langley Grove, 29
Langley Road, 29
Langley, Thomas, 29

Langtry, Lily, 53, 62, 76
Leatherhead Road, 43
Lewis, John, 72
Lime Grove, 58, 59
Liverpool, Earl of, 11, 58, 63, 68, 76
Liverpool Road, 76
London General Omnibus Company, 86
London Road, 12, 13, 21
London United Tramways, 47, 84, 85
London Zoological Society, 76
Long Ditton, 38, 39, 40
Longfellow Road, 97, 100
Lord Chancellor Walk, 69, 70
Louis-Philippe, King of France, 28
Lovekyn Chapel, 12, 13
Lovelace, Earl of, 40
Lovelace Gardens, 40
Lovelace Road, 40
Lower Ham Road, 14, 15, 24

Mackenzie-Grieve, Kenneth, 19
Malden Adult Education Centre, 52, 54, 55, 71
Malden and Coombe Borough Council, 49, 52, 65, 73, 94, 95
Malden and Coombe Civic Society, 52, 59, 73
Malden and Coombe Local Board, 51
Malden Branch Library, 50, 54, 61
Malden College, 71
Malden Fire Station, 52, 54
Malden Fountain, 50, 67, 100
Malden Green Common, 93, 94
Malden Manor Railway Station, 57
Malden Methodist Church, 55
Malden Parochial School, 71
Malden Police Station, 50, 54
Malden Road, 52, 55, 57
Malden Rushett, 44, 45, 46
Maldens and Coombe Urban District Council, 51, 53, 59, 65, 68, 94
Manor House East and West, 13
Maple Lodge, 29
Maple Road, 26, 29, 31
Market House, 2
Market Place, 2, 3, 4, 6, 10, 85

Mary, Adelaide, Duchess of Teck, 74, 77, 81
May, Princess, 74, 77, 81, 82
Maypole, The, 29, 40
Mecklenburg House, 49
Melba, 69
Merryweather, F. Somner, 50, 51, 68, 77
Merton College, Oxford, 43, 45, 53, 54, 90, 93, 94, 95
Merton Priory, 41, 68
Merton, Walter de, 89, 96
Metropolitan Convalescent Institute, 28, 48
Mill Street, 21
Millais, Sir John, 91, 92
Minerva Road, 22
Moor Lane, 44
Morley, John William, 99, 100
Mount Tavey, 91, 96
Muir, Annie, 45

National Society for the Protection of Young Girls, 28, 48
Native Guano Company, 23
New Malden Soup Kitchen, 60
New Victoria Hospital, 67
Nicols, Daniel and Celestine, 34, 35
Nightingale, Florence, 68, 79, 80
Nonsuch Palace, 45, 89, 90, 91
Norbiton Common, 48
Norbiton Hall, 13
Norbiton Park Hotel, 54

Oakhill, 33, 37
Oakhill, Crescent, 37
Oakhill Grove, 35, 37
Oakhill Road, 37
Oil Mill Lane, 46
Old Bridge Street, 22
Old Kingston Road, 45
Orchard Road, 3, 7, 9, 15
Organ Inn, The, 89
Orr, Canon Arthur Wellesley, 75
O'Sullivan, Father Eugene, 49, 50
Outrigger, The, 22

Paget, Lady Muriel, 66, 67
Park Farm (Malden), 49
Park Road (Kingston), 74
Park Road (Surbiton), 35

Parkfield, 63
Parr's Banking Company, 3
Patti, Madame Adelina, 34, 59
Pearson, James, 101
Pearson, Stanley, 100, 101
Penn Ponds, 73
Penny, Sir George, M.P., 32
"Perfume Parade", 23
Plough, The, 58, 78, 93
Plough Green, 58, 96
Pooley, Thomas, 30
Poplar Walk, 58, 59
Portsmouth Road, 25, 26, 27, 28, 29, 33, 38, 40, 92
Pratt's Alley, 9
Providence Place, 53, 58

Queen Elizabeth Grammar School, 12
Queen's Promenade, 15, 24, 28
Queen's Regiment (Surrey Office) and Museum, 26, 27

Railway Road, 25
Railway Hotel, 60
Railway Tavern, 30, 60
Raven's Ait, 35
Red Lion, The, 14
Regent Cottage, 34
Regent House, 34
Regent Road, 34
Regent Studios, 35
Richardson Evans Memorial Playing Fields, 88
Richmond Park, 71, 72
Richmond Road, 7, 14, 17, 18, 21
Ripon, Lady, 68, 69
Ripon, Lord, 64, 69
Rising Sun, The, 46
Robin Hood Farm, 81
Robin Hood Gate, 77, 78
Robin Hood Lane, 81, 82
Robinson, Sir Clifton, 84, 85
Rokeby School, 64
Rosebery Avenue, 71
Roselands Clinic, 48
Rossetti, Dante Gabriel, 91
Row Barge, The, 22
Rowlls Road, 7
Royal Avenue, 91
Royal Borough of Kingston upon Thames, Coat of Arms, 30, 54

Royal County Theatre, 16
Royal Eye Hospital, 29
Rythe, The, 38

St Agatha's Roman Catholic Church, 69, 75
St Andrew's Church, 31
St Anne's Roman Catholic Church, 75
St James's Church (Malden Road), 56
St James's Church (Poplar Walk), 51, 56, 59
St James's Close, 71
St James's Hall, 8, 28
St James's Road (Kingston), 4, 6, 7, 22, 28
St James's Road (Surbiton), 32
St John the Baptist Church (Kingston Vale), 77, 81, 82
St John the Baptist Church (Old Malden), 44, 45, 46, 56, 89, 90, 92, 94
St John the Divine Church, 56
St Joseph's Roman Catholic Church, 49
St Joseph's Roman Catholic Primary School, 7, 21, 98
St Luke's Church, 74
St Mark's Church, 30, 31
St Mark's Hill, 30, 31
St Mark's Memorial Cairn, 31
St Mary's Church (The Avenue), 90, 91, 96
St Mary's Parish Church (Long Ditton), 38
St Mary the Virgin's Church, 44, 45, 89
St Mary the Virgin's Mission Church, 44, 45
St Matthew's Church, 56
St Matthew's School, 38
St Matthew's School House, 43
St Nicholas' Churchyard, 39
St Paul's Church (Hook), 19, 41
St Paul's Church (Kingston Hill), 56, 74, 75
St Paul's National School, 41
St Peter's Church, 13, 48, 74
St Philip's Church, 90, 97
St Raphael's Roman Catholic Church, 28

Sandown Racecourse, 69
Seething Wells, 28, 29
Seething Wells Lane, 29
Sequire, 13
Shannon's Corner, 55, 82
Shepherd, Punch, 13
Sherman, J. A., 65
Sherriff, R. C., 35
Shrubsole Bank, 3, 26
Shrubsole Fountain, 3, 85
Shrubsole, Henry, 3
Shrubsole, Mrs John, 26
Siddal, Elizabeth, 91, 92
Smith, Rose Emma, 97
Smith, Walter Thornton, 65
Smith, William Shore, 79, 80
Sopwith Aviation Works, 17, 18
South Bank Lodge, 36
South Lane, 61, 95
Southampton Hotel, 25
Southborough House, 29
Spencer, Earl, 62, 68, 81, 89
Spicer, Graham Prockter, 50, 51, 52
Stag's Meadow, 42
Stapylton, Rev. William Chetwynd, 44, 46, 90, 94
Star, The, 46
Station Hotel, 60
Steadfast Sea Cadet Corps, 15, 16
Steptoe, Councillor Frank, 24, 73, 102
Sugden Road, 42
Sun Hotel, 3
Surbiton Adult Education Centre, 33
Surbiton Assembly Rooms, 26
Surbiton Borough Coat of Arms, 30
Surbiton Cottage Hospital, 31
Surbiton County Grammar School, 33, 37
Surbiton Crescent, 26
Surbiton Hall, 26
Surbiton Hill, 32, 33, 34
Surbiton Hill Park, 34
Surbiton Hospital, 31, 35
Surbiton Improvement Commissioners, 25, 26, 28, 29, 31, 32, 34
Surbiton Lagoon, 24
Surbiton Place, 28
Surbiton Police Station, 37

Surbiton Railway Station, 25, 30, 53
Surbiton Road, 25, 26
Surbiton Urban District Council, 31, 33, 42
Sycamore Grove, 58

Tangye, Derek, 64
Tangye, Sir Richard, 64
Taylor, J. W. R., 18, 19
"Teetotal Cottages", 32
Telegraph Cottage, 72, 73
Territorial Army and Volunteer Reserve Headquarters, 26, 27
Terry's Lane, 29
Thames Ditton, 38, 39, 40
Thames Side, 15
Thames Street, 3, 8, 12, 84
Three Compasses, The, 9, 78
Tiffin Boys and Girls Schools, 7, 21, 22, 98
Tolworth, 35, 37, 38, 45, 57
Tolworth Fountain, 37, 38
Town Hall (Market Hall), 2, 4, 67
Traps Lane, 67, 68, 82

Union, The, 48
Union Street, 5
United Kingdom Temperance Institution, 32
United Reformed Church, 10, 55
Upper Brighton Road, 29, 40

Veitches Nursery, 67
Victoria Avenue, 29
Victoria, Queen, 1, 4, 28
Victoria Recreation Ground, 32
Victoria Road, 29, 30, 31
Villiers Avenue, 26, 34, 46
Villiers, Barbara, 45, 90
Villiers, Sir Francis, 34
Villiers Road, 34, 46, 47

Wall, Max, 59, 60
Wall, Thomas, 36
Walpole Road, 25
War Memorial Gardens, 4

Warren House, 67
Warren Rise, 63
Warren Road, 66, 71, 72
Washington Road, 96, 97
Water Lane, 14
Way, Father William, 75, 76
Weeding, Thomas, 94, 95
Welbeck Close, 71
Wells, H. G., 92
Wesleyan Chapel (Malden), 55, 56
West-by-Thames Street, 1, 21
Westbury Road, 56
Weston Green Road, 33
White Lodge, 72, 74, 77, 81
White's Mineral Water Works, R., 17
Whiteoaks, 43
Wiles, Wilfred, 52, 59, 60, 73
Williams, Mrs Hufwa, 69, 70
Williams, John, 4
Wilson, Geoffrey, 83, 84
Wimbledon and Putney Commons Conservators, 88, 89
Wimbledon Common, 62, 88
Wimbledon Shooting Grounds, 97
Winey Hill, 42
Winter's Bridge, 38, 39
Wolsey, Cardinal, 1, 22, 45, 70
Wood, Alan, 94, 95
Wood Street, 14
Wood, The, 35
Woodfield Gardens, 57
Woodfield Hotel, 57
Worcester, Earl of, 91
Worcester Hotel, 99
Worcester House (Worcester Court), 93
Worcester Park Farmhouse, 91, 92
Worcester Park House, 91
Worcester Park Railway Station, 93, 94, 99, 101

Young, Leslie, 99
Young's Buildings Passage, 9
Youssoupoff, Prince Felix, 70

Zinkeisen, Doris and Anna, 43